The U.S. Congress established the East-West Center in 1960 to foster mutual understanding and cooperation among the governments and peoples of the Asia-Pacific region, including the United States. Officially known as the Center for Cultural and Technical Interchange Between East and West, it is a public, nonprofit institution with an international board of governors. Principal funding for the Center comes from the U.S. government, with additional support provided by private agencies, individuals and corporations and more than 20 Asian and Pacific governments.

The Center promotes responsible development, long-term stability, and human dignity for all people in the region and helps prepare the United States for constructive involvement in Asia and the Pacific through research, education, and dialogue. It provides a neutral meeting ground at which people with a wide range of perspectives exchange views on topics of regional concern. Eighty researchers pursue individual and cooperative projects, provide policy advice to Asian and American public and private agencies, and work with 275 Center-funded students from Asia, the Pacific, and the United States who are simultaneously enrolled at the University of Hawaii. Some 2,000 scholars, government and business leaders, educators, journalists, and other professionals from throughout the region annually work with the Center's staff to address topics of contemporary significance.

The Center focuses on four interconnected region-wide policy issues: post-Cold War regional security arrangements; social and cultural change; the domestic political evolution of Asian and Pacific nations; and rapid economic growth and its interrelated consequences (especially environmental concerns, energy needs, and demographic change).

THE PACIFIC ISLANDS:
Politics, Economics, and International Relations

Te'o I.J. Fairbairn
Charles E. Morrison
Richard W. Baker
Sheree A. Groves

East-West Center
Program on International
Economics and Politics

© 1991 The East-West Center International Relations Program
All rights reserved
Manufactured in the United States of America
Second printing 1993

Library of Congress Cataloging-in-Publication Data

The Pacific Islands: politics, economics, and
international relations
  / Te'o I. J. Fairbairn ... [et al.].
    p.   cm.
  Includes bibliographical references and index.
  ISBN 0-86638-140-6
  1. Islands of the Pacific—Politics and government.
2. Islands of the Pacific—Economic conditions. 3. Islands of the Pacific—Foreign relations. I. Fairbairn,
Te'o
DU29.P22 1991
990—dc20
                                        91-13100
                                            CIP

Cover design: Russell Fujita

This book is printed on acid-free paper and meets the
guidelines for permanence and durability of the Council on Library Resources.

Distributed by
University of Hawaii Press
Order Department
2840 Kolowalu Street
Honolulu, Hawaii 96822

Table of Contents

List of Tables and Maps	vii
Preface and Acknowledgments	ix
Introduction	1
Chapter 1 The Background and Leading Issues	3
Chapter 2 Pacific Island Politics	15
Chapter 3 Pacific Island Economies: Prospects for Development	39
Chapter 4 Regional Cooperation	65
Chapter 5 The Islands and the World	83
Chapter 6 The Pacific Islands in the Pacific Community	103
Appendix 1 Pacific Island Profiles and Maps	113
Appendix 2 Notes on the Leading Intergovernmental Regional Organizations in the Pacific Island Region	155
Appendix 3 Exchange Rates Per U.S. Dollar, 1983–1987	165
Index	167
About the Authors	171

List of Tables and Maps

List of Tables

Table 1.1	Pacific Islands: Selected Physical and Economic Indicators	6
Table 1.2	Political Status of Pacific Islands	10
Table 3.1	Pacific Island Economies: Domestic Exports by Value and Principal Products, 1988	47
Table 3.2	Aid Flows to the South Pacific, 1988	49

Statistical Notes: 1) All financial statistics are given in U.S. dollars unless otherwise noted. 2) Statistics for the Pacific islands have been derived from a variety of sources, and therefore in some cases figures may not be consistent.

List of Maps

The Pacific Islands	xii		Niue	132
American Samoa	112		Northern Marianas	134
Cook Islands	114		Palau (Belau)	136
Federated States of			Papua New Guinea	138
Micronesia (FSM)	116		Solomon Islands	140
Fiji	118		Tokelau	142
French Polynesia	120		Tonga	144
Guam	122		Tuvalu	146
Kiribati	124		Vanuatu	148
Marshall Islands	126		Wallis & Futuna	150
Nauru	128		Western Samoa	152
New Caledonia	130			

Preface And Acknowledgments

This book has been a joint effort by members of the Program on International Economics and Politics at the East-West Center, Honolulu. The principal author was Te'o Fairbairn, a Pacific economist who wrote chapter 1 on the general background to the Pacific region, chapter 3 on economics, chapter 4 on regionalism, the appendixes 2 and 3. Sheree Groves was the principal drafter of chapter 2 on politics. Charles Morrison authored chapter 5 on the international relations of the Pacific islands. Fairbairn and Richard Baker co-authored chapter 6 on the Pacific islands' relations with the Pacific Rim. Baker, with Groves, edited the entire manuscript for publication. Appendix 1's profiles of the Pacific islands were prepared by Sitiveni Halapua, Director of the Pacific Islands Development Program, and Groves.

The primary aim of this volume is to provide a succinct account of trends, issues, and recent developments affecting the Pacific islands in the political, economic, and international relations fields. The book was written for interested individuals in government, business, and academia, as well as students, who are looking for a broad introduction to this region which nevertheless takes an analytical approach to trends and developments. We believe this book fills a gap in the existing literature on the Pacific, and that it will make a contribution toward better understanding of the many complex issues that are now being confronted in this region.

The draft manuscript was reviewed by a number of distinguished Pacific island officials and scholars, and discussed at a July 1990 workshop in Suva, Fiji. Participant-reviewers from Suva were Asesela Ravuvu, director of, and Uentabu Neemia, research fellow at, the Institute of Pacific Studies, University of the South Pacific (USP) Suva, and Jioji Kotobalavu, director, South Pacific Applied Geoscience Commission (SOPAC). Additional comments were received from Siwa Siwatibau, director of the ESCAP Pacific Operations Center, Port Vila, Vanuatu; Leataua Kilifoti Eteuati, secretary to government, Apia, Western Samoa; Meleseini Faletau of the South Pacific Forum Secretariat's Economic Services Division; Michael Owens, deputy chief of Mission of the U.S. Embassy, Suva; and Ron May of Australian National University. Andrew Axline, chairman of the Department of Political Science, University of Ottawa, Canada, provided the background for the section on Papua New Guinea in chapter 2. Alan Ward, head of the History Department at the University of Newcastle, Australia, reviewed and commented on chapter 2.

The editorial and production team included Jacqueline D'Orazio, Dorine McConnell, and Dorothy Villasenor. Deborah Forbis copyedited the manuscript. The maps in appendix 1 were prepared by Brooks Bays, University of Hawaii, Hawaii Institute of Geophysics. The authors would like to express their gratitude for the valuable contributions made by these individuals, and at the same time exempt them from blame for any remaining deficiencies in the work.

Te'o I. J. Fairbairn
Charles E. Morrison
Richard W. Baker
Sheree A. Groves
Honolulu, January 1991

THE PACIFIC ISLANDS

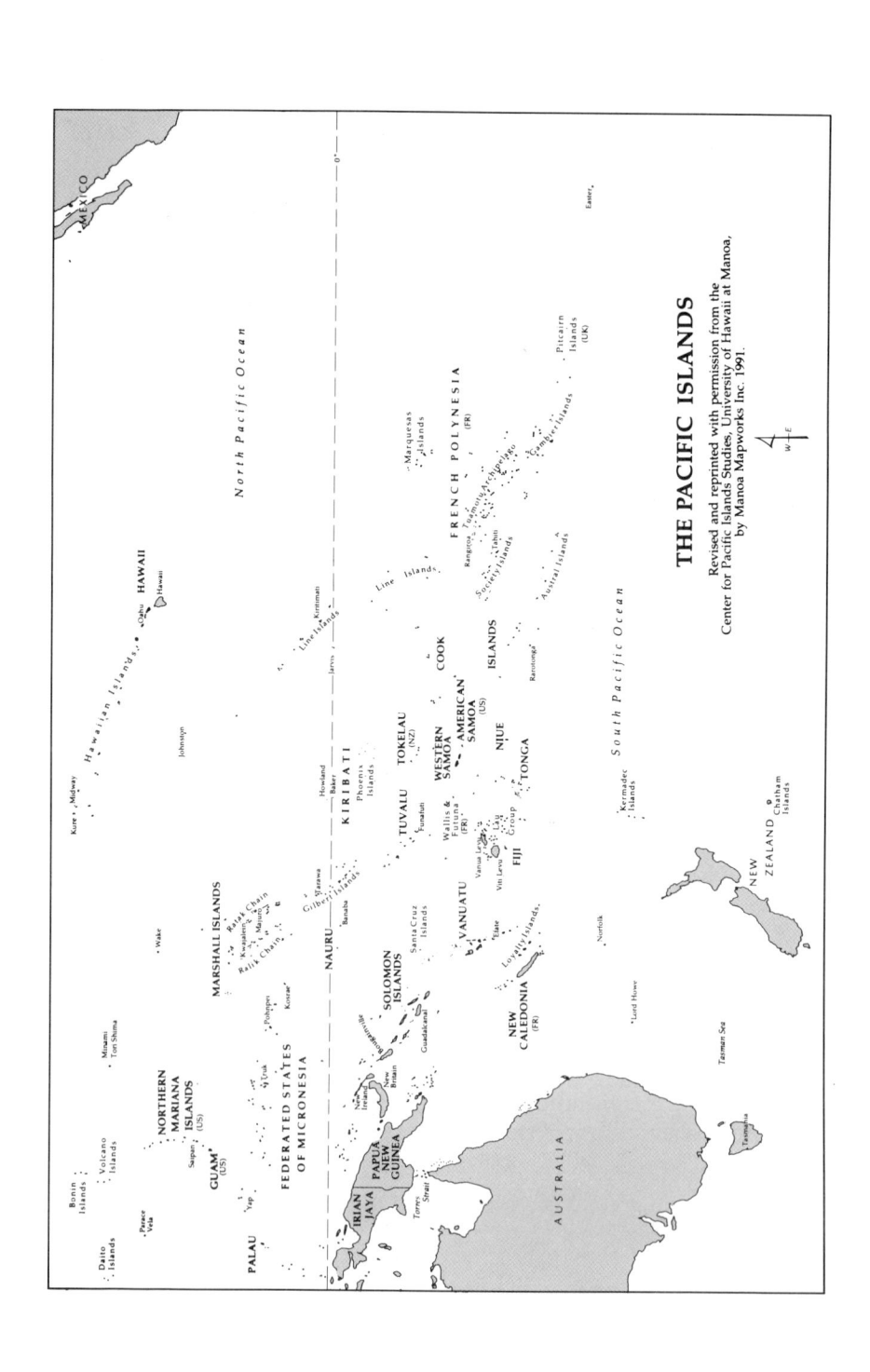

Introduction

At the dawn of what some see as the Pacific Century, the many small islands of the Pacific, scattered widely over the world's largest ocean, are going through a crucial phase of their history. Most have only recently recovered their independence, and are intensely involved in the essential tasks of nation building—pursuing economic development, developing their own political institutions and traditions, projecting their national identities, and expanding linkages with each other and with the rest of the world. They also face the challenges of dealing with greatly increased outside interest in their region, and of finding a place and role in the broader, dynamic Asia-Pacific region.

Traditionally regarded as a haven of calm and tranquility, the Pacific island region has entered a less settled phase. Particularly in the 1980s, the region experienced a series of disturbances and shocks—both internal and external in origin—that have significantly changed its character and attracted greater attention from the outside world. Among the sources of tension are communal differences, leadership and generational conflicts, the increased involvement of external powers, the independence issue in New Caledonia, opposition to French nuclear testing, and efforts to establish a regional nuclear-free zone. These and related issues reflect the emergence of a more complex world within which the many small island countries must make their way. Together, they add a dimension of uncertainty to visions of a "new Pacific."

This book is an introduction to the contemporary Pacific islands and the major issues this region faces in both the domestic and international spheres. The subjects of this discussion are the 21 Pacific island entities listed in table 1.1. (All these countries fall within the geographical and regional scope of the South Pacific Commission—a leading regional organization.) They include islands in the North as well as South Pacific. Irian Jaya, a province of the Southeast Asian state of Indonesia that constitutes the western half of New Guinea, is not included in the basic group but is mentioned at several points because of its indigenous Melanesian population and common border with Papua New Guinea. We do not deal with the Hawaiian Islands, despite the Polynesian heritage of the indigenous Hawaiian people, because of the very high degree of integration of Hawaii with the United States in social, political, and economic terms. Rapa Nui (Easter Island) and other

Chilean islands in the southeast Pacific are also not included because of the great distance and cultural gap between them and the other island entities. And finally, we do not discuss a number of miniscule islands (Norfolk, Johnston, Midway, Pitcairn, etc.) that have populations barely reaching into the hundreds and are totally dependent on the larger countries (Australia, the United States, the United Kingdom, etc.) with which they are affiliated.

The book provides basic information on each of the island entities and groups. It covers political structures and issues, prospects and constraints in their economic development, the state of regional cooperation, and major issues and trends in the political and international relations field.

Chapter 1 provides general background on the islands and surveys the major issues faced by the Pacific islands in the contemporary world. Chapter 2 discusses the political life of the islands, which have generally adapted well to democratic forms of government and are politically stable. Special attention is given to Melanesia, where politics have become more volatile in recent years.

Chapter 3 deals with the economies of the islands. Following an enumeration of the major constraints to development faced by the island entities, the chapter describes the main characteristics of the economies—their structures, national income, trade, and other foreign linkages. It concludes with a discussion of the prospects for growth, with special emphasis on the small resource-poor islands whose economic futures are particularly problematic. Regional cooperation is examined in chapter 4. It begins with an analysis of the nature of Pacific island regionalism and some of the imperatives and incentives underlying its evolution. It discusses the roles of the leading regional organizations, including the South Pacific Forum and the South Pacific Commission, and also points out certain areas where regional cooperation has not succeeded. An assessment of future possibilities for cooperation concludes the chapter.

Chapter 5 reviews Pacific island relations with the larger outside powers. Recent developments that have disturbed the region's tranquility are highlighted, including increased large-power rivalry and the international reaction to Fiji's 1987 military coups.

Chapter 6 provides a short survey of Pacific Basin economic cooperation, which to date has largely excluded the island region. This chapter discusses possible mechanisms for achieving more meaningful participation by the Pacific islands in the processes of Pacific economic cooperation. As an additional reference tool, appendix 1 provides short profiles and maps of all 21 Pacific islands. Appendix 2 provides further information on major intergovernmental regional organizations.

1
The Background and Leading Issues

THE PHYSICAL AND CULTURAL SETTING

The 21 political entities of the Pacific island region are spread—rather haphazardly—over the vast expanse of the Pacific Ocean, itself covering one-third of the earth's surface (see map). From the Northern Mariana Islands, at its northwestern limits, the region stretches through Micronesia and New Guinea, to New Caledonia and the Kingdom of Tonga along its southern perimeter and French Polynesia at its eastern extremity. The region encompasses an aggregate area of over 31 million square kilometers (km²), although only 551,400 km² of this is land.

Physically, except for Papua New Guinea, all the Pacific islands are small and many are miniscule, though due to their geographic dispersal some possess vast ocean Exclusive Economic Zones (EEZs). Papua New Guinea, which occupies the eastern half of the huge island it shares with the Indonesian province of Irian Jaya plus a number of smaller outlying islands, has a land area amounting to 462,840 km², equal to 83 percent of the region's total land mass (see table 1.1). Next to Papua New Guinea in size is Solomon Islands, with a total land area of 28,369 km². The majority of the remaining island groups have land areas that do not exceed 500 km² and at least three of them—Tokelau, Tuvalu, and Nauru—cover no more than 30 km².

Differences in geological structure and degree of dispersion are also notable. While all the Pacific islands are basically of volcanic origin, they fall into three physical-geologic categories: (1) complex serpentine formations—for example, Papua New Guinea, Solomon Islands, and New Caledonia; (2) high volcanic structures—such as the two Samoas and Rarotonga in Cook Islands; and (3) coral atolls—Tokelau, the Northern Cook Islands, Wallis and Futuna, and the Marshalls. Those in the first category are large and support a greater variety of land forms and natural resources. Mountainous and rugged terrain are common characteristics, and these features contribute to the fragmentation of population and the existence of a diversity of languages and sociocultural groups. The high volcanic structures are also physically diverse; like the serpentine islands, they are characterized by rugged mountain ranges, river systems, and some mineral resources but have much smaller land masses. The third category are tiny in size, low-lying (except for raised coral atolls such as Niue) and flat, and lack land-based resources of any significance.

Several Pacific island entities, such as Niue and Western Samoa, are relatively compact in the sense that they consist of only one or several closely contiguous islands (or islets). By contrast, many others consist of numerous islands—hundreds in some cases—dispersed over vast areas; examples of the latter type are Kiribati, French Polynesia, and the Federated States of Micronesia. Kiribati consists of 33 islands lying astride the equator and spread over 5 million km² of ocean, with the most distant outer island lying over 4,000 km from South Tarawa, the main island and national capital. Among other things, such an extreme degree of dispersion poses very difficult problems for transportation, administration, distribution of social services, and economic development in general.

The islands divide into three distinct cultural areas—Melanesia, Polynesia, and Micronesia. The Melanesian entities consist of Papua New Guinea, Solomon Islands, Vanuatu, and New Caledonia; Fiji straddles both Melanesia and Polynesia—ethnically predominantly Melanesian but with a strong cultural affinity to Polynesia. In this discussion Fiji is treated as part of Melanesia. The Melanesian entities are by far the most populous and rich in land and natural resources. There is great cultural diversity, with over one thousand languages spoken. In recent years consciousness of a Melanesian identity has sharpened, prompted partly by a wish to project a Melanesian viewpoint on issues of regional and international importance. The Polynesian islands—Cook Islands, French Polynesia, Western Samoa, American Samoa, Tokelau, Tonga, Tuvalu, and Wallis and Futuna—are physically smaller than the Melanesian islands and their resource bases are considerably thinner. The larger island groups such as Western Samoa and Tonga have adequate natural resources—both land and sea—to achieve a reasonably comfortable existence, but in the case of the atoll-based communities, most strikingly Tokelau and Tuvalu, scarcity of resources often reduces living conditions to basic subsistence. Limited development prospects have led to heavy aid dependence and pressures to migrate overseas.

The Micronesian islands—Kiribati, the Federated States of Micronesia, Palau (Belau), Guam, the Marshall Islands, Nauru, and the Commonwealth of the Northern Marianas—like the Polynesian entities are small, scattered, and generally resource-poor. Except for Kiribati and Nauru, all of Micronesia came under United States jurisdiction—Guam as a territory and the others under a United Nations trusteeship. Heavy aid dependency is characteristic, particularly for the United States-associated entities.

The population of the region currently (1990) totals just over 6 million. Actual population figures for 1987 show that out of a total regional population of 5.7 million, Papua New Guinea accounted for 3.5 million or 61 percent, and Fiji for 726,000 or 13 percent. This leaves the remaining islands with only 1.5 million or 26 percent (see table 1.1). Population densities also differ widely. They are particularly high for the small island countries, such as Nauru and Tuvalu with 419 and 327 people per km^2 respectively. The highest population density in the entire Pacific region is found in the tiny islet of Ebeye, on Kwajalein atoll in the Marshall Islands, where over 7,000 people live on 0.3km^2 of land. Next is South Tarawa in Kiribati with an estimated 1,350 per km^2 (Carter, 1984; 455).

Population growth averaging 1.9 percent per year, while high is below that of other developing regions—Africa, Latin America, and Asia. This situation reflects high birth rates combined with unusually low mortality rates that in turn reflect, among other things, major advances in public health measures. The population of Melanesia is growing particularly rapidly, but among several Polynesian countries, net growth rates in recent years have been kept low by heavy and sustained emigration. Mainly as a result of these high population growth rates, children comprise an unusually high proportion of the total population, producing relatively high dependency ratios.

Mobility is a notable feature of Pacific island populations, as reflected in movements from rural to urban centers, from outer islands to main islands, and overseas migration. Emigration has been a particularly major force among the Polynesian islands. Over the years, emigration has given rise to large Polynesian communities in such metropolitan cities as Auckland, Los Angeles, and Honolulu. It is believed that over 100,000 Samoans and 40,000 Tongans now reside overseas, while more Niueans, Tokelauans, and Cook Islanders live abroad than on their home islands.

RESOURCES AND ECONOMIC POTENTIAL

Pacific islands suffer from geographic isolation and dispersion and, except for Papua New Guinea, have small land masses and restricted resource endowments. Yet, looking beyond the constraining circumstances of individual cases, it should also be noted that the region as a whole enjoys certain natural advantages from which even the smallest

Table 1.1 Pacific Islands: Selected Physical and Economic Indicators

Country	Population 1987	Land area (km²)	Sea area (EEZ) (000 km²)	Density (people per km²)	GNP per capita 1988 (U.S. $)	ODA per capita 1988 (U.S. $)
American Samoa	36,700	197	390	186	5,277[b]	1,590[a]
Cook Islands	17,100	240	1,830	71	2,040[a]	631
Federated States of Micronesia	97,700	701	2,978	139	1,256[c]	450[d]
Fiji	725,500	18,272	1,290	40	1,540	58
French Polynesia	176,800	3,265	5,030	54	7,480[b]	1,715
Guam	119,800	541	218	221	5,470[b]	447[a]
Kiribati	67,700	690	3,550	98	650	176
Marshall Islands	37,800	179	2,131	211	1,317[e]	460[d]
Nauru	8,800	21	320	419	9,090[f]	—
New Caledonia	153,500	19,103	1,740	8	5,760[b]	1,653
Niue	2,500	259	390	10	1,080[f]	1,626
Northern Mariana Islands	20,600	471	777	44	9,170[b]	4,346[a]
Palau	14,000	494	629	28	2,420[b]	1,940[a]
Papua New Guinea	3,463,300	462,840	3,120	7	820	84
Solomon Islands	292,000	28,369	1,340	10	430	117
Tokelau	1,600	10	290	160	560[f]	1,446
Tonga	94,800	699	700	136	800	128
Tuvalu	8,500	26	900	327	453[b]	1,585
Vanuatu	145,000	11,880	680	12	820	195
Wallis and Futuna	14,700	255	300	58	750[f]	1,540[a]
Western Samoa	162,000	2,935	120	55	588	113
Total/average	5,660,500	551,452	29,523	10.3		

a 1987   e 1984
b 1985   f 1980
c 1983   — not available
d 1986

Notes: 1. Population estimates were provided by the South Pacific Commission.
2. National income figures for American Samoa, Cook Islands, Fiji, and Guam are for GDP.
3. National income figures for FSM apply to the Trust Territory of the Pacific Islands.
4. See appendix 3 for exchange rates.

Sources: Asian Development Bank (1987), Australian National University (1988), South Pacific Commission (1986), International Monetary Fund (1988), World Bank (1987), Fairbairn (1985), Siwatibau (1990).

entities can sometimes benefit. The region contains substantial deposits of certain key minerals such as gold, copper, and nickel. Papua New Guinea is already a major producer of gold and copper, as is New Caledonia of nickel. Major oil discoveries have been made in Papua New Guinea. The recent declarations of Exclusive Economic Zones under the Law of the Sea Conventions have meant that the Pacific islands now control the largest fisheries (mostly tuna) in the world. Many if not most of the islands have significant potential in tourism based on their natural beauty and distinctive cultures. Also, both the region's remoteness and its geographic spread have given it strategic value to external powers (whether for bases, activities such as weapons testing, or simply denial of access to others) which in turn has brought financial aid and other forms of assistance.

From the viewpoint of resource endowment and development potential, the Pacific islands can be divided into four major categories:

The first group comprises the relatively large island groups—Papua New Guinea, Fiji, Solomon Islands, New Caledonia, and Vanuatu—which have the best resource potential. Together these account for an estimated 84 percent of the region's total population of 6 million, and each possesses extensive land areas for agriculture while several also have control over large EEZs. These resources provide a basis for major development in agriculture, forestry, fisheries, and tourism, and in one or two cases, minerals. Much progress has already been made in developing this resource potential, and this has contributed toward the achievement of a relatively high measure of diversification and economic growth.

The second group are the middle-sized islands, represented by Western Samoa and Tonga, which have modest resource bases. Agricultural potential is present but constrained by limited land areas. EEZs are small (Western Samoa has the smallest EEZ in the region), commercially exploitable minerals are absent, and tourism has only limited scope. Paucity of raw materials and small domestic markets restrict industrialization and therefore also limit economic diversification.

French Polynesia also falls in this group in terms of land-based resources, but differs from Tonga and Western Samoa by its high geographic dispersion and control over a vast EEZ (the largest in the region). Its strategic value to France has led to a substantial inflow of external funds (both as aid and as military expenditure), and this combined with a large tourist industry has made for high levels of money income. Because of these special features, French Polynesia has much in common with the fourth group of islands discussed below.

The third group comprises the small, remote, and resource-poor islands—Kiribati, Tuvalu, Niue, Tokelau, and Cook Islands. These all have limited land-based resources, and also lack the capacity to exploit their EEZs although they are among the largest in the region. Agriculture is at a low level and restricted almost entirely to subsistence production. Opportunities for industrial development are negligible, and only one or two of these countries can attract tourists. Economic diversification is rudimentary as exports are dominated by a single traditional crop, mainly copra.

A fourth possible grouping encompasses several small islands that enjoy some singular advantage that compensates for otherwise poor economic prospects. These special-case economies include Nauru, which is overridingly dependent on lucrative though soon to be exhausted phosphate deposits; Palau, Guam, the Marshall Islands, and the Commonwealth of Northern Marianas, whose strategic value to the United States enables them to benefit from large financial subsidies; and American Samoa whose location and good harbor have allowed it to become a major fish processing center. Through the exploitation of these special assets, these entities have been able to raise their living standards to levels that are among the highest in the region.

For the larger islands—and especially Papua New Guinea—prospects for significant economic growth based on the exploitation of their natural resources are bright. The situation facing the smaller resource-poor islands is a stark contrast: many of them for the foreseeable future will depend, precariously, on their capacities to identify and develop specialist "niche" economic activities and, at the same time, on the continued goodwill of the international aid community.

POLITICAL AND SOCIAL ISSUES

Of the 21 Pacific island entities, 15 have populations under 100,000, and 5 have populations under 10,000. Thirteen are independent or self-governing; half of these gained their independence since 1975. Clearly these are some of the smallest, newest, and therefore most fragile polities in the world.

The achievement of political independence was an issue of overriding significance for most Pacific island countries during the postwar period. Western Samoa, which became independent in 1962, was the first Pacific island to do so. The decolonization process accelerated in the 1970s, with six island countries attaining independence or self-government over the decade. Today, nine Pacific island countries enjoy independence, while four others are self-governing in free association with their respective former colonial authority (see table 1.2). Of the remaining dependent territories, one (Palau) is moving toward free association status (though with difficulty); the future status of the other seven dependencies is not clear. The most controversial of these is New

Table 1.2 Political Status of Pacific Islands

Current or Former Colonial Power	Independent Nation	Self-governing in Free Association	Continued Dependent Status
New Zealand	*Western Samoa (1962)	Cook Is. (1965) Niue (1974)	Tokelau
United Kingdom	*Fiji (1970) Tonga (1970) Tuvalu (1978) *Solomon Is. (1978) Kiribati (1979) *Vanuatu (1980)		
Australia	Nauru (1968) *Papua New Guinea (1975)		
France	*Vanuatu (1980)		French Polynesia New Caledonia Wallis & Futuna
United States		Marshall Is. (1986) Federated States of Micronesia (1986)	American Samoa Guam Commonwealth of No.Mariana Is. Palau

* = United Nations Member

Notes: 1. Years in parentheses indicate dates independence or free association was achieved.

2. Vanuatu appears twice in the list of independent nations as it was jointly ruled by the United Kingdom and France.

3. Tonga signed a Treaty of Friendship and Protection with the United Kingdom in 1900, but was not administered as a colony. The United Kingdom over-saw Tonga's foreign affairs until 1970 when Tonga reentered the comity of nations.

Source: Hamnett and Kiste, 1988: 10.

Caledonia, whose political life has been marked by violence in recent years.

The political systems in the islands are diverse and include one monarchy, one military-installed government, parliamentary and presidential-type arrangements, and various forms of territorial administration. Generally, the transition to self-government has been smooth, and most of the island states have adopted political systems based on a melding of local tradition and British-style parliamentary government.

By and large the postindependence history of the region has also been characterized by political stability. However, in a number of cases there have been subsequent challenges to the constitutional arrangements, and pressure to align them more closely to local traditions. The personalistic nature of leadership in the islands and the relative newness and weakness of fiscal control systems have also contributed to patterns of pecuniary politics and corruption and thus to a degree of political volatility in some cases. In addition, ethnic and regional differences have led to increasing instances of political tension and conflict in recent years.

In common with other traditional societies, the Pacific islands have also experienced profound changes in their social, economic, and political life as a result of interaction with the outside world. To an increasing extent—as outside contacts have intensified—the islanders have had to come to terms with forces of change: to take up the challenge of development and modernization, to modify traditional economic systems, to improve health and education, to establish regional and international links, and to protect and adapt valued aspects of their traditional cultures. At the same time, these challenges—and the responses they have elicited—have imposed tremendous strains on the social life of many Pacific islands. Among the many complex problems are the steady drift of rural populations to urban centers, high rates of unemployment, disruption to established family systems, increasing incidence of "Western-type" diseases and, in some cases, rising rates of youth suicide.

The rural-to-urban migration syndrome is widespread and reflects many closely interrelated motivations—the desire for employment and education, the attractions of urban lifestyles ("the bright lights") and, often, a wish to escape from the rigidities and restrictions of traditional rural life. The consequences have often been far-reaching: the loss of rural population has seriously undermined the social and economic viability of many rural communities including the outer islands. In urban centers, the growing populations have strained public facilities and services, led to overcrowding and the spread of shantytowns, caused breakdowns in family life, and swelled the ranks of the unemployed. Other associated problems include increased crime and drunkenness, and a deterioration in dietary standards that often results in serious malnutrition and increased vulnerability to disease.

Finding productive jobs for expanding populations is crucial for most Pacific island countries. Job opportunities have tended to grow at rates well below the expansion of the labor force, while additional pressures are created by the rural-to-urban flow. Sustained emigration has eased the pressure for some islands, but this solution itself creates other social (and economic) problems. Current development programs in the islands characteristically emphasize employment creation through economic expansion as well as manpower training to enhance the employability of the labor force, but they have given little attention to population control policies. The employment issue remains particularly intractable for the small, resource-poor island states, such as Kiribati and Tuvalu, that have no established emigration outlets.

Nonetheless, almost all these islands have made substantial progress in tackling the many social problems. With a few exceptions, notably in Melanesia, significant progress has been recorded in reducing infant mortality rates (and with it the overall death rate) and in extending life expectancy. In the majority of cases, enrollment rates for children of primary school age are high, and this accomplishment has resulted in unusually high literacy rates.

REGIONAL AND INTERNATIONAL LINKAGES

The Pacific islands have much to gain from regional cooperation. Such cooperation can make for a more efficient use of resources and give the islands a more powerful voice in dealing with the larger countries outside the region. It has also provided a vehicle, particularly through regional conferences, for Pacific island leaders to discuss issues of regional significance and to do so in their own unique style—the "Pacific Way," based on consensus, mutual respect, and regard for the needs of all.

Regional cooperation among the islands has progressed as far as in any developing region. Regional organizations have been established to serve a variety of needs: to provide a forum for political leaders, to improve economic, social, and cultural services, and to facilitate cooperation in the diplomatic-international arenas. Specialist agencies are active in key functional fields such as shipping, fisheries, the environment, and offshore exploration for minerals. In developing these organizations, the approach has been pragmatic, favoring regional efforts in areas that bring direct and tangible benefits to participating island countries. Forms of cooperation that call for tight integration of the economic and political life of the region have not been pursued.

Pacific island regionalism is still evolving, and in recent years appears to be undergoing a process of consolidation and self-appraisal, often involving tension and controversy. Some Pacific islands feel that there is excessive duplication in the work of the major regional bodies, a condition that needs to be corrected. Cleavages between the Melanesian and Polynesian islands, and between the smaller and the larger islands have also surfaced. Yet, despite these and related problems, regional cooperation remains fairly robust; certainly it has achieved much in providing practical services valued by island members and in promoting regional interest in the wider world.

On the international front, the Pacific has been increasingly affected by the involvements of external powers, which have required new responses and, in some cases, led to ill-feeling and resentment. The single most significant new development was the Soviet effort in the mid-1980s to negotiate fisheries access treaties with island entities. The activities of United States fishing fleets in the region created much friction and bitterness in the early 1980s, but the underlying issue was resolved by the negotiation of a regional fisheries access treaty. Other issues stemming from foreign involvements in the region have included nuclear and other weapons testing, dumping and related environmental threats such as toxic waste disposal, and remaining decolonization questions.

Large-power competition has raised the profile of the Pacific on the international stage. In particular, the Soviet initiatives led the large Western powers, especially the United States and Japan, to review their own policies toward the region. The United States significantly scaled up its diplomatic representation and somewhat expanded its development assistance. Japan has promised substantially more aid and is seeking to find appropriate uses.

Generally, the Pacific islands have succeeded in establishing effective links with traditional donors—both bilateral and multilateral—for purposes of securing financial and technical assistance. In fact, on a per capita basis the region ranks among the highest aid recipients in the world. Trading channels with traditional partners, such as Australia and New Zealand, are also well developed. However, economic relations with the larger countries of the Asia-Pacific Rim, including Japan and the newly industrialized economies—the so-called NIEs—have been limited. Closer economic interaction with these dynamic East Asian economies is worth exploring, for the potential benefit to the Pacific islands would seem to be significant.

REFERENCES AND SUGGESTED READING

Asian Development Bank. *Key Indicators of Developing Member Countries of ADB.* Vol. XVIII (July), Manila, 1987.

Australian National University. *Pacific Economic Bulletin*, Vol. 3, No. 1 (June), National Center for Development Studies, Canberra, ACT, 1988.

Carter, J., editor. *Pacific Islands Year Book* (15th edition). Pacific Publications, Sydney, 1984.

Fairbairn, Te'o I. J. *Island Economies: Studies from the South Pacific.* Institute of Pacific Studies, University of South Pacific, Suva, 1985.

Hamnett, Michael P. and Robert C. Kiste. "Issues and Interest Groups in the Pacific Islands," a study commissioned by the U.S. Information Agency (USIA), Research Office, December 1988.

Hegarty, David. "International Relations and Security in the South Pacific," paper presented at the Conference on ASEAN and the Pacific Islands (September 1987) East-West Center, Honolulu.

International Monetary Fund. *International Financial Statistics.* Vol. XLI, No. 9 (September 1988), Washington, D.C.

Morrison, Charles E., editor. *Asia-Pacific Report: Trends, Issues, Challenges, 1987–1988.* Chapter 5: "The New Pacific Island States," East-West Center, Honolulu, Hawaii, pp. 57–70.

Siwatibau, Siwa. "The South Pacific Countries and Regionalism," unpublished paper presented at the symposium on Cooperation in Asia and the Pacific, East-West Center, Honolulu, 1990.

South Pacific Commission. *Overseas Trade 1983.* Statistical Bulletin No. 27, Noumea, 1986.

World Bank. *The World Bank Atlas 1987* (20th edition), Washington, D.C., 1987.

2
Pacific Island Politics

INTRODUCTION

The Pacific island region was the last major region of the world to be decolonized. The transition from colony to full independence or greater self-government has been relatively slow, peaceful, and democratic.

Still relatively young—most have been politically independent or self-governing for less than 20 years—the Pacific island nations are now having to deal with larger, more complex issues in the region than the domestic problems they faced in the early years of independence and self-government. A new generation that is more outspoken and better educated is dissatisfied with the status quo and is pressing for solutions to the low standard of living caused by economic difficulties compounded by isolation. Ethnic, regional, and cultural differences are fueling political instability. These domestic challenges coupled with external concerns occupy the political agenda of the region.

The 1980s have been especially volatile: coups in Fiji, riots in French Polynesia and Vanuatu, escalated violence in New Caledonia, increased lawlessness in Papua New Guinea, and a guerrilla war on Bougainville Island. This chapter will examine the political development of the Pacific islands and current trends.

COLONIZATION

By the early twentieth century the Western powers (the United Kingdom, the United States, Germany, the Netherlands, Spain, and France) in their international scramble for territory and influence had completed colonization of the Pacific island region. All islands had been annexed or had become protectorates by 1906 when France and the United Kingdom established a joint "condominium" over the New Hebrides (now known as Vanuatu).

Colonial control of some of the islands changed hands during the first half of the twentieth century. The Spanish-American War in 1898 ended Spain's hold in the region, as Micronesia was divided between the United States (Guam) and Germany (what now comprises the

Northern Marianas, the Marshalls, the Federated States of Micronesia, and Palau). The Samoas were divided between the United States (American Samoa) and Germany (Western Samoa) in a 1899 treaty in which the United Kingdom withdrew its interests in these islands in exchange for German concessions in Tonga, Niue, and Solomon Islands. After World War I, Germany went the way of Spain, losing control of its Pacific island territories. Under a tripartite League of Nations mandate, Australia, the United Kingdom, and New Zealand took over the administration of Nauru, which had been a German protectorate since 1888. New Zealand acquired control over German Western Samoa at the outbreak of the war, while Japan gained Germany's Micronesian islands. After the defeat of Japan in World War II, the United States took control of Micronesia under a United Nations trusteeship.

Solomon Islands, Kiribati and Tuvalu (formerly the Gilbert and Ellice Islands, respectively), and Fiji remained under United Kingdom control until the 1970s. The New Hebrides continued under joint British-French rule until its independence in 1980. The United Kingdom turned over administrative control of Niue and Cook Islands to New Zealand in 1901. And Tokelau, a United Kingdom protectorate from 1877, became a territory of New Zealand in 1925.

By the start of the twentieth century, the island of New Guinea was divided between the United Kingdom (the southeast region known as Papua), Germany (the northeast region, or New Guinea), and the Netherlands (Netherlands New Guinea, or West Irian). In 1905, Australia took possession of Papua from the United Kingdom, German New Guinea came under Australian administration during World War I, and after the war a League of Nations mandate confirmed the former German colony under Australian control. After World War II, a United Nations trusteeship was established aiming at eventual independence and unification of both Papua and New Guinea, and Australia was appointed as trustee. West Irian remained under the control of the Netherlands until it came under the UN Temporary Executive Authority in 1962. Indonesia took over in 1963, eventually incorporating the region as a province in 1969 and renaming it Irian Jaya in 1973.

THE COLONIAL LEGACY

The populations of most Pacific islands are small and, except for Guam, Niue, and Nauru, each island group is made up of a collection of islands and islets that are widely scattered over a vast area with great cultural and linguistic differences. The small size of most communities and their isolation from each other not only limited the extent to which people could meet and organize, but also encouraged affiliations to villages and regions which inhibited development of a national base for independence movements. Prior to World War II, only Western Samoa, with a long history of resistance to colonial rule, had a genuine indigenous independence movement.

The 1960 UN Declaration on the Granting of Independence to Colonial Countries and Peoples accelerated global decolonization, and by 1965 only a few dependent territories remained. However, concern over smallness and limited economic resources slowed the decolonization process in the islands. Also, the options of integration or free association with another state in many cases offered attractive alternatives to full independence.

The colonial powers had taken differing approaches to administrative control in their colonies, granting varying degrees of local autonomy. These administrative approaches, as well as the nature of the individual societies to which they were applied, determined the pace and extent of the decolonization process.

Those societies that were more cohesive and less scattered geographically, like the Polynesian islands of Tonga and Western Samoa, were able to resist external control more effectively. Tonga was the only island group that was not formally colonized, having signed a Treaty of Friendship and Protection with the United Kingdom only in 1900, and was not administered as a colony. Under the treaty, the United Kingdom oversaw Tonga's foreign affairs until 1970. Western Samoa was the first of the island groups to gain full independence in 1962.

While the Polynesian cultures are relatively homogeneous, Melanesia consists of highly diverse, culturally fragmented societies. Both Polynesia and Micronesia have aristocratic, hierarchical social structures with traditional authority vested in chiefs, while in Melanesia the social structure is more egalitarian, with authority and status usually based on skills and achievement. In Tonga and Western Samoa these traditions continue to play a major role in politics. In other Polynesian and Micronesian societies, constitutional and other privileges are still granted to chiefs, although their role may only be in an advisory capacity or limited to traditional matters and customs—such as the House of Ariki of Cook Islands, and the House of Iroij in the Marshall Islands.

The British colonizers (including Australia and New Zealand) utilized the traditional systems as a framework for colonial rule. Islander legislative councils were first established to act in advisory capacities to the colonial administrations. These advisory councils ultimately evolved into elected and appointed parliaments. It is noteworthy that all nine Pacific island states that achieved full independence between 1962 and 1980 are former British colonies.

However, independence was not achieved without struggle. Western Samoa as early as the 1920s pushed for independence. The Mau of Pule movement, founded in 1908, first resisted German rule and then in the 1920s opposed New Zealand control, eventually achieving limited self-government under a UN trusteeship. In 1947 New Zealand instituted constitutional legislation that led to full Samoan independence in 1962. Nauruans had already begun preparations in the 1950s for independence from their UN trustees, Australia, New Zealand, and the United Kingdom, through the establishment of the Nauru Local Government Council. By 1966, a legislative council was set up with a large measure of self-government. Complete independence followed two years later, and Nauru became a republic.

In Papua New Guinea (PNG), concerted preparations for independence from Australia began only in the 1960s, when Australia felt pressure from the growing numbers of ex-colonial states in the UN. In 1964, the first general election was held for the House of Assembly. The process of establishing self-government steadily accelerated, and full independence was granted in 1975. Nineteen provincial governments, each with its own elected assembly, executive council, and premier, were established by constitutional amendment in 1976.

The decline of British power after World War II, withdrawal from "East of Suez" after 1967, and entry into the European Economic Community in 1973 contributed to the U.K.'s supportive approach and active facilitation of moves towards independence for its Pacific colonies. The decade of the 1970s saw full sovereignty returned to Tonga (1970) and full independence gained by Fiji (1970), Solomon Islands (1978), Tuvalu (1978), and Kiribati (1979).

While the British preserved the traditional ruling systems, the French by contrast followed a practice of assimilation aimed at replacing the traditional authorities with their own, and pursued a colonial policy centered on the French metropolitan government. None of the French territories, with the exception of Vanuatu that was under French-British condominium, has gained full independence. Only recently, after the dramatic events in New Caledonia discussed below, has France held out the possibility of greater independence for any of its remaining Pacific territories, which also include Wallis and Futuna, and French Polynesia.

Joint rule of Vanuatu resulted in rivalry between the colonizing powers for indigenous loyalties and support, and a split between Anglo-Protestant and Franco-Catholic segments of the local communities. The British-backed New Hebrides National Party, now the Vanua'aku Pati, sought independence in opposition to the French-backed Union of Moderate Parties (UMP). Independence was ultimately achieved in 1980, but not without violence—a separatist movement on the northern island of Espiritu Santo and the southern island of Tanna was quelled only after Papua New Guinea troops were called in to support the new government.

Where both the British and the French had explicit colonial policies, the United States never developed a theory of colonial rule. Politically, the U.S. territories are governed under a system based on the U.S. federal structure that balances national and local interests. All the U.S. island territories have opted now for a self-governing status, with the U.S. government exercising direct control only over defense and security-related issues.

Under the UN Trusteeship Agreement of 1947, the U.S. Micronesian territories formed the Trust Territory of the Pacific Islands (TTPI), consisting of the Marshall Islands, the Northern Marianas, Palau, and the Federated States of Micronesia (formerly the Caroline Islands). The UN anticipated that the islands would remain as one political unit after the trusteeship ended. However, the islanders thought otherwise. Although TTPI islanders belong to the Micronesian grouping, differences in language and traditional customs exist, and there was a long precolonial history of autonomy on the part of the four island groups.

The people of the Northern Marianas launched a campaign to become a commonwealth in 1976, and the United States agreed to split the territories. The Federated States of Micronesia (FSM), the Republic of the Marshall Islands, and the Republic of Palau all in turn negotiated Compacts of Free Association (CFA) with the United States that were approved by the U.S. Congress and signed into law by President Ronald Reagan in 1986. However, the political future of Palau's CFA is still uncertain. A conflict remains between the Palauan constitution's antinuclear provisions and U.S. defense rights under the compact. The U.S. government has taken the position that the CFA cannot be implemented and the trusteeship status terminated until the Palauan constitution is reconciled with the compact. On 22 December 1990 the UN Security Council voted to dissolve the 43-year-old UN Trusteeship over the Northern Marianas, Marshall Islands, and FSM, leaving Palau as the only remaining part of the Trust Territory.

POLITICAL SYSTEMS

Independent Island States

The independent Pacific island states, whether fully independent or self-governing, generally have adopted governmental systems modeled on the structure and processes of their metropolitan power. The former British colonies have modified forms of the British model for their constitutional framework. All have elected parliaments, but with variations in electoral arrangements. Except for Tonga, which is ruled by a monarchy, the heads of government are elected by parliament; with the exception of Western Samoa, Nauru, Kiribati, and Fiji, the head of state is a governor-general appointed by the British queen upon the advice of the prime minister or government. In Western Samoa the Parliament appoints the head of state and does not acknowledge the queen. All are members of the Commonwealth, with the recent exception of Fiji which was excluded when it became a republic following the coups in 1987.

In most of these island nations, executive power resides in a cabinet headed and selected by a prime minister who is either the head of a political party or is directly elected by parliament from among its members. The cabinet is selected from members of parliament or from political parties within parliament, resulting in a government answerable to that body.

Both Western Samoa and Tonga operate to a substantial degree on traditional precedents. Under Western Samoa's constitution, the head of state must be chosen from holders of the four paramount titles, and 45 of the 47 members of the country's unicameral parliament were traditional chiefs, or *matai*, who were elected by their peers—other titled Samoans; while the remaining two members of Parliament were non-Samoans elected by universal suffrage from rolls of individual voters. An October 1990 referendum changed this, allowing universal suffrage for Samoans 21 years or older. However, it remains that only *matai* can be candidates for 45 of the 47 parliamentary seats. In Tonga, the constitutional monarchy in 1875 established a Privy Council as the highest executive body, headed by the king, with ministers and two governors appointed by the king. In the 28-seat Legislative Assembly, 9 members are elected by popular vote, another 9 are nobles elected by the aristocratic families, and the remaining 10 are appointed by the king with cabinet rank. The cabinet is headed by a prime minister.

The republics of Nauru and Kiribati both have presidents as head of state. In Kiribati the president is also the head of government, and in Nauru he is the de facto prime minister. Both presidents are elected from among nominated members selected from and by the members of parliament.

In the more fragmented societies of Melanesia, Solomon Islands and Papua New Guinea governments have slowly become more decentralized. Solomon Islands is divided into 8 provincial governments, and Papua New Guinea has 19 provincial governments each with its own elected legislature and premier.

Fiji, which had been invaded by Tonga prior to European arrival, developed a Polynesian-style traditional hierarchy of hereditary chiefs who still play an important role in politics. From the time of independence in 1970 up until the coups of 1987, Fiji was governed by a parliamentary democracy. In a multiracial country where indigenous Fijians were at the time a minority, constitutional legislation preserved a balance between the Fijians, Fiji Indians, and other racial groups. The prime minister was chosen by majority vote in the lower house of a bicameral parliament consisting of an elected House of Representatives and a Senate. The members of the Senate were nominated by the Great Council of Chiefs, the prime minister, the Council of Rotuma, and the leader of the opposition. In postcoup Fiji, a new draft constitution was promulgated in July 1990 to provide stronger guarantees of indigenous Fijian political supremacy.

Fiji, Vanuatu, Cook Islands, and Western Samoa all have well-developed political party systems. The other island states, however, despite their adoption of the British model, lack cohesive parties. Fiji's ethnic sensitivities are evident in the development of its main precoup political parties: the Alliance Party, the dominant party since independence, consisting of a majority of ethnic Fijians; and the National Federation Party, dominated by Fiji Indians. This latter party merged with the urban-based Labour Party for the April 1987 election, which brought to power for the first time an Indian-dominated government.

In Vanuatu, regional sentiments are strong and parties are mainly split along the lines of colonial affiliation: the Vanua'aku Pati (Anglo-Protestant) and the Union of Moderates (Franco-Catholic). Recently, however, new parties have emerged in Vanuatu: the trade union-backed Labour Party, the educated young professionals' New Peoples' Party, and the National Democratic Party. In 1988, due to rivalry between members of the ruling Vanua'aku Pati, that party split, creating the New Melanesian Progressive Party.

Parties in Solomon Islands and Papua New Guinea are characterized primarily by shifting alliances centered around prominent individual figures. Western Samoa shares this characteristic to some degree, in that parties are fluid and based on individuals and organizations. However, Western Samoa's parties are less fragmented, due to that country's long tradition of a closely knit society in contrast to PNG's and Solomon Islands' cultural diversity and lack of a strong national identity.

Solomon Islands and PNG also share the same voting system: single-member constituencies and a "first-past-the-post" rule whereby the candidate with the most votes wins even if the total falls short of a majority. In PNG this system, combined with the large number of candidates running for office, allows for members of parliament to be elected on the basis of quite small percentages of the vote. Party switching and tribal conflicts between supporters of opposing parties often erupt after elections. This fragility of party allegiances also means that governments have to depend upon coalitions to remain in power. During the course of a coalition's life, policy differences are settled by compromise and bargaining. However, personalism, localism, and regionalism dominate politics as each group seeks to gain what it can, leading to persistent parliamentary instability.

Voting in Solomon Islands runs largely along personal and regional lines. The Parliament has seen a high turnover of members in the three elections since 1978. In the most recent election, in March 1989, 257 candidates contested 38 parliament seats.

Political parties have been absent in Tonga, Tuvalu, Kiribati and, until recently, Nauru. In these island nations, the cabinet acts as the government and the rest of parliament acts as an "opposition." As a result, decisions are often made through consensus.

Self-Governing States

In most cases, the islander communities have not wished to lose the benefits of financial aid and the other opportunities available through ties with the metropolitan power. This is evident both in the continued close relationships between the fully independent states and their former colonizers, and in the number of island entities that have chosen the status of "self-governing in free association" instead of full independence: Cook Islands (1965) and Niue (1974) in association with New Zealand; the Federated States of Micronesia, the Marshall Islands, and Palau (Belau) with the United States. The Northern Mariana Islands have a similar status under another name: they constitute the self-governing Commonwealth of the Northern Marianas in union with the United States under a covenant.

Although the essence of the free-association relationships with the United States and New Zealand is the same, there is a difference in the legal basis in each case. In Cook Islands and Niue, association status is written into their constitutions. Association can only be repealed by a constitutional amendment endorsed by a two-thirds majority vote of the islands' legislative assembly in a referendum. New Zealand assumes responsibility for the defense of both, and foreign affairs for Niue; Cook Islands now essentially runs its own foreign affairs.

The FSM, Marshall Islands, and Palau association arrangements are the product of treaties delegating defense rights and responsibilities to the United States and committing the United States to provide financial and other assistance. The commonwealth covenant granting internal self-government to the Northern Marianas also gives the United States control over defense and foreign relations. The treaties acknowledge the sovereignty of the island states, and they formally became members of the international community upon the dissolution of the UN trusteeship in December 1990. They have the right to terminate the Compact arrangements on the expiration of the agreed period (15 years).

As with the independent island states, the freely associated islands have adopted political systems modeled on those of the metropolitan powers. The British parliamentary system serves as a model for New Zealand's freely associated states of Niue and Cook Islands. Niue, consisting of a single raised atoll, has a Legislative Assembly of 14 members representing individual village constituencies, and another 6 elected at large by popular vote. The first Niuean political party, the Niue People's Action Party (NPAP) was formed in 1987.

Cook Islands, with constituents scattered across seven northern atolls and eight larger southern islands, is characterized by political fragmentation. Parliament consists of 24 members representing single-member constituencies. Politics have been significantly destabilized by party switching, with communities split among multiple parties. There were five successive governments and two general elections in 1983 because of factionalism and the inability to achieve consensus on issues. Since then there have been four prime ministers, with the latest elections having taken place in January 1989.

The U.S.-associated states adopted the presidential form of government, with differing specific structures. The Northern Marianas' governing body has a bicameral legislature composed of elected members in the House of Representatives and in the Senate. The head of government is an elected governor, and the head of state is the U.S. president. The Republic of the Marshalls, on the other hand, incorporates British as well as U.S. elements. The legislative branch of government is the Nitijela (parliament), which is advised by the Council of Iroij (local chiefs). The parliament elects a president from among its members.

Marshallese culture has a complex clan system from which political factions have developed. Traditional loyalties to family and party hinder groups from working together, and local issues rather than broad programs become the focal point of politics. Similar factional rivalries also characterize Palauan politics. Palau's Council of Chiefs still plays an advisory role to the president on traditional laws and customs, but the government is modeled after U.S. representative assemblies—a bicameral legislature composed of a House of Delegates and a Senate. Both the president and vice president of Palau are elected by direct popular vote.

The Federated States of Micronesia (FSM) comprises four island states: Pohnpei (Ponape), Truk, Yap, and Kosrae. Each, except for Kosrae, has several islands within its group. There is a wide range of cultural and linguistic attributes within these island states, and each has its own constitution and government, headed by a governor. A 14-member unicameral federal congress, the governing body, is located in Pohnpei, the capital of FSM. Each of the four state governments has 1 representative in this congress; the other 10 members are elected directly, on the basis of population, for two-year terms. This federal congress elects a president and vice president.

Palau's political status remains in limbo. It continues as the world's last UN trusteeship under U.S. administrative authority because of repeated failure of referenda to change Palau's constitution in a way that would meet U.S. requirements in the Compact of Free Association. Seven referendums have been held on the compact, the most recent having taken place in February 1990; all have failed to yield the constitutionally required 75 percent majority vote necessary to amend the constitution. As of mid-1990 the Palauan legislature was considering legislation that would amend the 75 percent requirement.

Dependent Territories

A few of the island entities remain territories under the control of the colonial power: Guam and American Samoa under the United States; the French territories of New Caledonia, Wallis and Futuna, and French Polynesia; and New Zealand's Tokelau.

Both Guam and American Samoa were governed by the U.S. Navy until 1951, at which time the Department of the Interior took over administrative control. Both territories have a popularly elected governor under the overall direction of the Department of the Interior. However, Guam has a unicameral legislature of senators elected by four districts, while American Samoa incorporates chiefly traditions into its political structure. In American Samoa's bicameral legislature, or Fono, the Senate consists of members elected under Polynesian custom by chiefly Samoan families and is made up of *matai* (traditional chiefs), whereas the House of Representatives is elected by popular vote.

In Guam, in recent years there has been movement towards greater autonomy. In 1987 the populace voted to seek Commonwealth status within the United States, along the lines of the Northern Marianas system. Although not advocating full independence, many Guamanians see Commonwealth status as offering a greater degree of home rule and increased economic freedom.

New Zealand's remaining territory, Tokelau, is made up of three atolls, each with its own administration run by an elected commissioner and village mayor, and with a Council of Elders as the dominant political unit at the village level. Ultimate authority lies with the New Zealand Ministry of Foreign Affairs that appoints an administrator and an official secretary. Seven directors responsible to the official secretary administer the various government departments.

France's three Pacific territories are each governed by the Government Council, headed by a French high commissioner and with members selected by the Territorial Assembly—the legislative arm—which is elected by popular vote. The three territories are represented in the French National Assembly by elected deputies (two each from French Polynesia and New Caledonia, and one from Wallis and Futuna) and one senator each. Each territory also is represented in the French Economic and Social Council.

The traditional chiefly system is still very much a part of politics in Wallis and Futuna. The senator, elected by the Territorial Assembly by majority vote, and the deputy, elected by universal suffrage, who represent the islands in Paris, are linked to the royal chiefly family of Wallis and Futuna.

RECENT TRENDS AND PROSPECTS FOR THE FUTURE

The Pacific islands' political systems are still in a transitional stage and are experiencing adaptation pains. The adoption of Western political models mixed with traditional aspects has given rise to a number of problems. The personalistic nature of the political cultures has contributed to a "revolving-door" characteristic of island politics. Loyalties to clan and region often override national interests, and there can be a fine line between what is viewed as corruption by Western standards and island cultural traditions of leaders' obligations to clan and family. Economic underdevelopment and uneven distribution of wealth have placed increased importance on money. This combination of personalistic politics and the issue of wealth has produced problems of corruption. For example, a Solomon Islands auditor-general's report (August 1989) raised questions about the non-accountability of funds received from the European Community. The Cook Islands government of Pupeke Robati was dogged by allegations of corruption, abuse of parliamentary allowances, and misappropriation of funds during 1987–88. At the time of his suicide in August 1988, former Palau President Lazarus Salii was under U.S. congressional investigation for allegations of bribery, corruption, mismanagement of funds, and drug trafficking. Subsequently, in August 1989 a U.S. General Accounting Office report questioned Palau's fundamental ability to manage itself given evidence of budget deficits, cash flow problems, debt, and improper spending.

Since the emergence of party politics in the political life of Western Samoa, there has been a scramble for increasing the number of *matai* in politics because the constitution limits membership in parliament to *matai* (except for two members on the commoner-individual voter rolls). As a result *matai* titles have been newly designated to people courting them for political reasons.

Generational changes taking place in the islands have added other pressures. A younger generation not satisfied with the status quo is calling for change. In the hierarchical, aristocratic societies of Polynesia and Micronesia, where the elders and chiefs are the greatest beneficiaries of wealth and power, these problems are most evident. In Tonga, for example, commoners are challenging the traditions of political power resting in the hands of the noble families. In September 1989, 6 ordinary (commoner) members of the Legislative Assembly, after a two-week boycott, presented a motion for major constitutional change. They called for reducing the number of noble representatives in the assembly from 9 to 3, increasing the number of members elected by popular vote from 9 to 15, and allowing ordinary members to introduce legislation. An additional motion called for an amendment to the constitution to provide for a two-party parliamentary system.

The action by the commoner members was a protest against what they considered misuse and waste of public funds by the aristocratic elite, taking place at a time when the country was facing difficult economic problems. In a system where the nobles always vote with the government, the commoners' motion would have created a genuine mechanism for checking the performance of the government. The 15 February 1990 election saw the reelection of the main leader of the commoner legislators, Samuela "Akilisi" Pohiva, by an overwhelming majority, indicating that the commoners as a group are not satisfied with the present system and are seeking more democratic representation and greater accountability by government leaders.

Land and Ethnicity

Underlying all these debates and conflicts are issues of land and ethnicity which have traditionally been critical factors in the lives of the Pacific islanders. Today they continue to play an important role in the social and political arenas. Of the three main cultural groupings, Melanesia has emerged as an area of particular volatility: two coups in Fiji, a determined independence movement in New Caledonia, a failed rebellion in Vanuatu, and the convulsive politics of Papua New Guinea. Root issues of land and ethnicity, or regional differences, can be found behind all these events.

In all Pacific island cultures there is a deep emotional attachment to the land. Land tenure holds social, economic, and political importance to the islanders, and is central to feelings of self-worth and security. Land-use and distribution rights are tied to traditional kinship and social relationships. They are a source of political power by which the traditional chiefly systems are sustained. Prior to Western contact, land was communally owned and transferred through inheritance or warfare. Land could be made available to others for use, but it belonged to the clan in perpetuity.

Colonial domination changed the traditional patterns by introducing private land ownership and commercial exploitation. Alienation of land by Western colonization aroused feelings of dispossession and loss of identity for the indigenous peoples. Agitation for the return of alienated land was a cause of unrest under colonial rule and played a role in independence movements. The prevention of land alienation was one of the major reasons behind the earliest Pacific constitution—the Tongan Constitution of 1875. Island leaders, during their quest for independence in the 1960s and 1970s, used constitutional legislation to correct the alienation suffered under colonial rule and preserve indigenous land ownership.

Land issues remain very much a concern for the Pacific nations. In Nauru, the most pressing current issues revolve around the exploitation and destruction of the land through years of phosphate mining, started under German colonization in 1907 and continued under the UN trustees—Australia, New Zealand, and Britain. Mining has left the island a virtual moonscape, and Nauru has begun legal proceedings in the International Court of Justice to gain compensation from the former trustees for loss of land and royalties. In Guam, the indigenous Chamorros voted in favor of the Guam Commonwealth Act in 1987 largely out of concern over losing control of their land to outsiders. The act, now under U.S. congressional review, includes a provision requiring the United States to pay for 44,300 acres (about one-third of Guam's total land area), which it uses for military and federal purposes. More recently, in Papua New Guinea, disputes over land compensation have produced a number of violent confrontations between landowners and government.

As elsewhere, colonization of the Pacific islands did not take into consideration ethnic and regional diversities. Different groups were often lumped together under a single colonial administration. The decolonization process stimulated a resurgence of cultural and ethnic pride, and in some instances tried to "correct" the lumping together of diverse groups under colonial rule. Thus, Niue split from Cook Islands (although the two were never formally united, they shared a common administration under New Zealand); the Micronesian Trust Territory fragmented; and Polynesian Tuvalu separated from Micronesian Kiribati. In addition, decolonization stirred secessionist efforts, as demonstrated by Bougainville Island's move to split from Papua New Guinea at the time of independence.

In some island nations ethnicity has played a major role in political alignments. On an individual island basis, such alignments can be seen in the political parties of Fiji—the Melanesian-backed Alliance Party and the Indian-dominated National Federation Party—and in New Caledonia's Melanesian-supported Kanak Socialist National Liberation Front (FLNKS) and the European-dominated pro-French, or anti-independence, Rally for New Caledonia in the Republic (RPCR). On a transnational basis, such ethnic alignments are evidenced by regional formations such as the Melanesian Spearhead Group comprising Papua New Guinea, Solomon Islands, and Vanuatu, and proposals for a corresponding Polynesian grouping to include French Polynesia, Cook Islands, Niue, American Samoa, Western Samoa, Tonga, and Hawaii (see chapter 4).

In the fragmented societies of Melanesia and Micronesia there are also sharp political divisions within ethnic groups based on cultural, language, or regional differences. Examples are the clan rivalries of the Marshall Islands and Palau, and the regional differences played out in the party politics of Solomon Islands and Papua New Guinea. In the cases of Vanuatu and Kiribati, cleavages left by colonialism continue to divide loyalties: Francophone and Anglophone rivalries in Vanuatu, and church-based rivalries between the northern Catholic-dominant and southern Protestant-dominant areas of Kiribati split communities and election results.

Conflicts stemming from political-economic domination of the indigenes by the settler population have increased. These tensions create political instabilities, and have played a part in the growth of indigenous political movements—the Taukei Movement in Fiji, the Polynesian Liberation Front in French Polynesia, and the FLNKS in New Caledonia.

In Irian Jaya, internal migration from other parts of Indonesia has given impetus to the Free Papua Movement. An indigenous Melanesian independence movement, the Free Papua organization operates along the border with Papua New Guinea. Although the movement has lacked efffective support locally and internationally, Irianese refugees crossing the border into Papua New Guinea have caused friction between that country and Indonesia.

While there is no independence movement in Wallis and Futuna, where politics focus largely on local issues, in both French Polynesia and New Caledonia there are independence movements that have become more active in recent years. In French Polynesia the independence movement, the Polynesian Liberation Front, is relatively small and is split between the majority who desire internal self-government with gradual independence, and a minority who are pressing for immediate independence. Those supporting continued French association fear losing French economic aid and the comparatively high standard of living that comes with such aid. However, social tensions have increased because of a rising cost of living and unemployment. A leading opposition figure in the Territorial Assembly, Gaston Flosse, has called for a free-association arrangement similar to that between New Zealand and Cook Islands.

The Polynesian Liberation Front's popularity among the indigenes has been aided by the growing economic and social gaps between the races. The economic successes and political advances of the French, Chinese, and those of mixed race are seen as a threat by the Polynesians who make up about 65 percent of the population. These tensions culminated in a riot in late 1987 when striking dockworkers protesting their growing workload rampaged through the streets of the capital of Papeete on the island of Tahiti, causing extensive damage. The economically and politically disadvantaged groups may increasingly be attracted to a pro-independence and even violent stance.

New Caledonia

Of all the Pacific territories, New Caledonia has been the most troubled. The New Caledonian independence movement is well organized and strongly entrenched among the indigenous Kanak population. The territory is split politically between the Kanaks, now a minority of the population (43 percent), who want independence, and the immigrant settler population. The settlers, or loyalists, are themselves a polyglot group, consisting of ethnic French (including refugees from former French colonies of Vietnam and Algeria), descendants of Javanese and Tonkinese laborers brought in to work the nickel mines, and islanders from Wallis and Futuna, but all want to remain a part of the French republic and fear a political takeover by the Kanaks. The loyalists dominate the economy of New Caledonia, and control Noumea, the main urban center and capital.

The Kanaks were part of a multiracial movement for local self-government during the 1960s. However, in the 1980s they intensified their struggle for independence from France and the restoration of sovereignty over their land. In 1980, Jean-Marie Tjibaou was elected vice president of the Government Council, the governing body of New Caledonia. This was the first time a Melanesian had reached such a political level. From 1980 to 1984, while Tjibaou was vice president, negotiations between the New Caledonia Government Council and France failed to reach a compromise on an interim statute for independence. The Melanesians consolidated their political organization under the Kanak Socialist National Liberation Front (FLNKS), a coalition of seven pro-independence parties with Tjibaou as president.

The FLNKS boycotted the elections of November 1984. Violence erupted and 10 people from Tjibaou's tribe were ambushed and killed; a number of the settlers involved in the ambush were also killed. To prevent further conflict, the French government negotiated the Pisani-Fabius plan recommending the creation of four regions that would administer themselves freely through regional councils elected by universal suffrage. In the September 1985 elections, the FLNKS won a majority of seats in three of the four regions—giving them a majority in the next New Caledonia Territorial Assembly. Only the southern region, where Noumea is located, was won by the pro-French Rally for New Caledonia in the Republic (RPCR).

However, when the election of March 1986 brought to power in France the conservative Prime Minister Jacques Chirac (with a slim majority importantly dependent on the votes of overseas conservatives such as the RPCR), the Pisani-Fabius plan was abolished. A new plan—the Pons Statute—was formulated with a new referendum that gave only two choices to New Caledonians: total independence or remaining a territory of France. The option of independence in association with France was eliminated, thereby alienating mainstream voters.

Although the FLNKS boycotted the September 1987 referendum, 59 percent of the eligible population voted, with the majority favoring the status quo. A new statute was adopted in the French parliament granting a form of internal autonomy to New Caledonia that December. However, the law created electoral boundaries that guaranteed control of at least two of four regions by pro-French settlers. This was perceived by the Kanaks as stripping them of their political, social, and economic gains, and was seen as ultimately undermining Kanak culture by redefining inalienable land under the French constitution as land that could be sold or transferred to non-Kanaks. When this law was passed, the Kanaks responded by taking French hostages, which in turn led to French paramilitary reprisals.

The threat of an all-out civil war in New Caledonia prompted, and the 1988 French elections enabled, the French government to reopen dialogue between the divided communities. In June 1988, under the leadership of the new Socialist Prime Minister Michel Rocard, RPCR leader Jacques Lafleur and FLNKS leader Tjibaou met in Paris and agreed on a four-point framework to avoid further bloodshed. Under the Matignon Peace Accords, France will continue to rule New Caledonia until 1998, when another referendum will be held. In the interim, New Caledonia is divided into three partly self-governing provinces (Loyalty Islands, the South, and the North), and elections in June 1989 set up new provincial assemblies and territorial congresses. As designed in the accords, two of the three provinces are now under the control of the Kanaks—the North Province and the Loyalty Islands—while the Southern Province is governed by French loyalists. Under the accords, France is also pursuing an economic and social development plan focusing on the underdeveloped Kanak areas and accelerating the training of Kanak public servants.

The accords appear to enjoy majority support in the Melanesian movement, due in part to Tjibaou's personal prestige and stature in the Kanak community. However, his assassination in May 1989 by Kanak opponents of the accords left a vacuum in the moderate leadership of FLNKS and raised new uncertainties about the future.

Fiji

Ethnic conflicts and their repercussions are not limited to the territories. In Fiji, two coups in 1987 released long pent-up ethnic tensions and ended what had been regarded as an exemplary model of democratic rule in a multiracial country. The first coup, in May 1987, followed the victory in a national election two months earlier of a coalition government in which Indian elements predominated. Although led by an ethnic Fijian, Labour Party leader Timoci Bavadra, the coalition consisted of the Indian-backed National Federation Party and the Labour Party, a multiracial middle class-professional party with a slightly greater Indian component. The former ruling Alliance Party, led by Prime Minister Ratu Sir Kamisese K. T. Mara since independence in 1970, was multiracial in composition, including Fiji Indians, but ethnic Fijians predominated. To many ethnic Fijians, the 1987 election allowed the Fiji Indian community to gain political ascendency over the indigenous Melanesians.

In the nineteenth century during the British colonial period, Indian indentured laborers were brought into Fiji to work the sugar plantations. Their descendants came to dominate trade, the civil service, and the professions in Fiji. Racial segregation under colonial rule had reinforced feelings of difference between the Fijians and Indians, and when the Fijians perceived a transfer of power to the Indian community, racial tensions finally erupted.

The 14 May coup was led by Lt. Colonel Sitiveni Rabuka of the Fijian army, who claimed he sought to avoid racial violence by ousting the Bavadra government. The coup was supported by the Great Council of Chiefs and the Taukei (Landowners) movement, based on perceived threats to Fijian interests. Of special concern to the Fijians was an apparent challenge to their land rights: the 1970 constitution provided safeguards of Fijian customary land ownership, but the Bavadra government had undertaken to examine the question of land rights of Indian farmers who leased land.

After the 14 May coup, an interim government headed by Governor-General Ratu Sir Penaia Ganilau was established to write a new constitution limiting the political role of the ethnic Indians. Later in the year, on 25 September, following a week of rising racial turbulence and anticipation that Ganilau was forming a bipartisan government to again share power with the Indian community, Rabuka staged a second coup. Rabuka revoked the 1970 constitution, declared Fiji a republic, and asked Ganilau to serve as president. With Ganilau's acceptance of the presidency, Fiji ended a 113-year association with the British Crown when it was excluded from the Commonwealth.

Fiji has since returned to civilian rule under Ganilau, who asked Ratu Mara to be prime minister. A draft constitution to ensure Melanesian political dominance was approved by the interim cabinet in September 1988. A 16-member committee selected by the president and comprising the different groups reviewed the draft in October 1988. The draft proposed a unicameral parliament where Melanesians would dominate. The president is to be appointed by the Great Council of Chiefs and has emergency powers. The draft constitution also called for separate voting registers and constituencies for the ethnic groups—Melanesian, Indian, Rotuman, and others.

The committee representation was criticized at the time by many Indian political leaders and the coalition. Bavadra, who has since died and been replaced by his wife Adi Kuini as head of the coalition National Federation Party, was not represented in the committee—although coalition members were invited to participate as individuals but declined. Bavadra rejected the draft, saying it discriminated not only against non-Fijians but also urban Fijians and those in the western regions. (Allocation of 37 parliamentary seats based on the population distribution in 14 provinces and 5 urban constituencies give Fijians in the east a higher level of representation and discriminates against coalition supporters. Furthermore, in the allocation of seats, urban areas are underrepresented compared to rural districts.) Also, substantial numbers of Fijians would prefer a constitution that gave Fijians even more power.

Recommendations by the constitutional review committee were released in September 1989. These recommendations were reviewed by the cabinet and by the Great Council of Chiefs and were promulgated by the president in July 1990. The committee recommended a two-house parliamentary system with 70 seats, the majority (37) for indigenous Fijians, and the scrapping of provisions giving the commander of the armed forces (then Rabuka) a permanent place in the cabinet.

Prime Minister Ratu Mara, who planned to retire in December 1989, agreed to stay on as prime minister until the new constitution is in place and elections held in 1991, while General Rabuka resigned his cabinet position, to return to his military duties. However, he continued to comment frequently on political matters, and in April 1991 it was reported that he would resign from the military and be appointed deputy prime minister. The opposition continues to threaten to boycott any election.

Vanuatu

While the conflicts in New Caledonia and Fiji have been race-related, those of both Vanuatu and Papua New Guinea are based on regional differences. Although the population of Vanuatu is mostly ethnic Melanesian, linguistically and culturally it is fragmented. There are nearly one hundred distinct languages and dialects. These differences are exacerbated by cleavages left from the chaotic and fractious British-French "pandemonium." Prime Minister Walter Lini and his Anglophone supporters are from the north, while his rival Barak Sope, his supporters, and the Francophone-dominated Union of Moderates Party (UMP) are from Efate, where the capital Port Vila is located, and nearby islands. Forty percent of the 140,000 population is French-speaking. The Francophones, discriminated against in education and employment, resent what they see as an unfair dominance of top positions and politics by people from the north island.

The most recent drama in Vanuatu politics included the jailing of the president, the secretary-general of the ruling party, and the opposition leader for attempting to overthrow the government. This upheaval began during the November 1987 elections in which ruling Vanua'aku Pati Secretary-General Sope unsuccessfully challenged Prime Minister Lini. Subsequently the Vila Urban Land Corporation (VULCAN), which managed land leases on behalf of customary owners was abolished after an audit showed a misappropriation of funds. This action was interpreted as a political attack on Sope who headed VULCAN.

Sope branded the closure as an assault on the Vanua'aku Pati and the constitution that guarantees that all land belongs to customary owners (except for "national land" which the government, with owner consent, can take over for public purposes). Sope was able to capitalize on the sensitive land ownership issue to launch a counterattack through a land rights protest in May 1988 that went out of control and erupted into rioting involving two thousand villagers in Port Vila. However, the riot only cost Sope his cabinet seat as minister of immigration and tourism. Later in July, Sope was expelled from parliament with four others after voting with the opposition UMP on a no-confidence motion. A boycott of parliament by 18 other UMP members to protest the expulsions resulted in their being sacked as well. Sope responded by forming the new Melanesian Progressive Party (MPP) in October of that year, and this party along with the UMP boycotted the December by-elections held for the vacant 23 (of a total 46) parliament seats.

The conflict peaked in December 1988 when President George Sokomanu (Barak Sope's uncle) attempted to fire Lini and his cabinet, dissolve parliament, and appoint a five-member interim government with Sope as prime minister and the UMP leader as deputy prime minister. Sokomanu, claiming he was acting to restore democracy after the opposition boycott led to Vanua'aku Pati domination of parliament, also urged the police and paramilitary forces to give allegiance to Sope. The troops did not defect, Lini had the president arrested, and the Supreme Court ruling found Sokomanu had no power to dissolve parliament and install a new government. Sokomanu, Sope, and the UMP leader were tried and convicted of mutiny, acting on personal ambitions and craving political power. Subsequently, however, the Vanuatu Court of Appeals released the three on the grounds of insufficient evidence, possibly setting the stage for still further maneuvers. But at the most basic level, with the overwhelming majority in parliament now supporting the northern Anglophones, regional tensions are likely to increase still further.

Papua New Guinea

Since Papua New Guinea is the largest country in the Pacific islands region, with the largest population and the greatest resource endowments, its political developments naturally attract more interest than most island countries. To date, PNG has offered a successful example of the British style of democracy in the region. However, the cultural and regional context in PNG prevents the system from operating with great continuity or stability, and the fact that all governments have been coalition governments and that coalitions have been fluid continuously threaten the stability of the government. At the electoral level, voting in PNG is determined overwhelmingly by particularistic loyalties rather than party labels, and thus no party has ever been able to obtain a majority of parliamentary seats. Currently nine parties are represented in parliament, and these groupings are based on regional and personal loyalties rather than ideology or program.

Compounding this fragility is a constitutional limitation allowing the opposition to move a vote of no-confidence once every 6 months, which could result in a change of government but not necessarily national elections. Any government thus can only be assured of a very short time in which to put its programs into effect before it can face potential defeat on a no-confidence motion brokered on purely opportunistic grounds. Despite this inherent governmental instability, PNG has had only four prime ministers since independence in 1975. But there remains continual fear that the tendency to defeat governments on votes of no-confidence could lead to government breakdown or failure to implement required long-term policy steps, leading ultimately to the collapse or overthrow of democratic institutions. The PNG parliament has been considering a bill that would amend the constitutional motion of a no-confidence vote by extending the 6 month period to 18 months.

Social and economic changes are placing further strains on the political system. Tribal warfare and urban violence in the form of personal attacks, theft, assassination, burglary, and rape have resulted in a law and order problem of sufficient severity that the government has made its solution one of the paramount goals of national policy. Organized gangs of youths, known as "rascals," are behind much of the disorder, a problem exacerbated by high unemployment among young men in the face of increasingly visible differences in wealth between the elite and the majority of the population.

The issue of distribution of wealth also lies behind growing demands by PNG landowners for more compensation for the rich mineral and oil deposits mined from their land. Royalties are normally allocated 95 percent to the provincial governments and 5 percent to the landowners. In 1988, industrial violence erupted at two major mining projects—Ok Tedi in Western Province and Bougainville Copper in North Solomons. In the former case, the issue was housing and suitable compensation for mine workers; in the latter it was claims for billions of dollars in compensation for landowners. Both cases resulted in rioting, looting, and sabotage that led to the closure of the mines and capital losses in millions of dollars.

Nor are these isolated cases. At the Porgera Gold Mine in Enga Province and the Hidden Valley Gold Mine, landowners have also demanded increased compensation. The PNG government realizes the importance of the mining industry to economic development and is now asking the provincial governments to offer higher royalty payments to landowners to avert more violence. The question has been raised whether the constitution gives landholders ownership of all minerals beneath their land. Some politicians and owners are arguing for tighter controls on foreign companies exploiting the oil and mineral deposits. There is also discussion of allowing landowners to hold equity in mine projects, which would mean they also would have to pay for a share of the costs and face the chances of losses.

The case of Bougainville, however, has special attributes. Along with the problems of landownership are ethnic, geographical, historical, and personality complications. North Solomons Province, where Bougainville Island is located, is the richest of all PNG provinces. Along with the copper mine, cocoa and copra plantations flourish. Despite these rich resources, however, government funding for infrastructure improvements and development has been negligible. Immigrants from other areas of PNG, including the Highland Provinces, have come in to work the plantations and mine. This has contributed to tribal tensions, particularly between the Bougainvilleans and highlanders.

Bougainville Island is geographically located only a few kilometers from the rest of Solomon Islands, while it is hundreds of kilometers from the PNG mainland. Bougainvilleans are ethnically different from the mainlanders—black as opposed to the mainland "red skins." Historically they have seen themselves as being apart from the rest of PNG, and have traditional ties with Solomon Islanders. There had been allegations of arms smuggling into Bougainville for the rebels from Solomon Islands.

The issue of secession was raised in the recent unrest starting in late 1988 by landowners of the Bougainville copper mine. A group of militant landowners led by Francis Ona, a former surveyor with the mine, broke away from the established Panguna Landowners Association that accepted the government's peace plan and offers of compensation in September 1989. Attacks by the rebel group, known as the Bougainville Revolutionary Army (BRA), led to the closure of the mine, declaration of a state of emergency on the island, and the movement of riot police and army troops into Bougainville to quell the rebels, reopen the mine, and end tribal conflicts that had erupted between highlanders and Bougainvilleans. The police and army presence, however, only added to the crisis, with increasing complaints by villagers of police and army brutality. The conflict moved into the plantation sector of Bougainville, and the situation was exacerbated by "rascal" elements primarily involved in criminal activity.

The guerrilla war between the BRA and PNG government police and army forces escalated until mid-March 1990 when a cease-fire monitored by a team of international diplomats came into force. The Papua New Guinea government and the secessionist rebels reached an agreement in January 1991 aimed at ending the conflict, but the future political status of Bougainville remains unresolved. As PNG undergoes further rapid economic and social changes, such challenges will pose a greater test to the existing system of parliamentary institutions.

CONCLUSION

Inevitably the pace of change will lead to more pressures, instability, and volatile politics in the Pacific islands. No region of the world has experienced the transition to independence without such problems, and the Pacific islands are no exception. However, the region does have strengths that should aid it in weathering this passage: the generally small scale of its polities, relatively strong traditional cultures and values, political traditions that stress consensus, good external relationships and corresponding access to assistance, and an absence of border conflicts or other serious disputes between the states.

REFERENCES AND SUGGESTED READING

Brigham Young University. *The Politics of Evolving Cultures in the Pacific Islands.* Honolulu: Institute for Polynesian Studies, February 1982.

Carter, John, editor. *Pacific Islands Year Book.* 15th edition. Sydney: Pacific Publications, 1984.

Cole, Rodney V. *Land Policies and Issues in the South Pacific.* Canberra: National Center for Development Studies, Australian National University, 1986.

Crocombe, Ron. *The South Pacific: An Introduction.* Langman Paul in association with the University of the South Pacific, Suva, 1983.

Davidson, J.W. *The Decolonization of Oceania: A Survey 1945-1970.* Wellington: New Zealand Institute of International Affairs, 1971.

Fry, G.E. *South Pacific Regionalism: The Development of an Indigenous Commitment.* Canberra: Australian National University, 1979.

Ghai, Yash. "The Making of Constitutions in the South Pacific: An Overview" in *Pacific Perspectives: Rethinking Pacific Constitutions.* Vol. 13, No. 1, pp. 1-33. Fiji: South Pacific Social Sciences Association, 1984.

Institute of Pacific Studies, University of the South Pacific. *Politics in Polynesia.* Vol. II of Politics in the Pacific Islands series. Suva, 1983.

Institute of Pacific Studies, University of the South Pacific. *Micronesian Politics.* (Revised edition of *Politics in Micronesia*), Vol. III of Politics in the Pacific Islands series. Suva, 1988.

Maiava, Iosefa A. "Issues of Politics in the Pacific Islands: An Overview," paper prepared for the Conference on ASEAN and the Pacific Islands, East-West Center, Honolulu, September 1987.

McDonald, Hamish. "Matters of Survival" in the *Far Eastern Economic Review* (15 October 1987), pp. 18-20. and "Alienation of Land is the Crucial Fear," pp. 20-22.

Morrison, Charles E., editor. *Asia-Pacific Report, 1987-88.* Chapter 5: "The New Pacific Island States," pp. 57-70. East-West Center, Honolulu.

Morrison, Philip S. and Murray Chapman, editors. A special issue of *Pacific Viewpoint*, Vol. 26, No. 1, April 1985.

Premdas, Ralph R. and Jeff S. Steeves. *Decentralization and Political Change in Papua New Guinea, the Solomon Islands, and Vanuatu*. Suva: University of the South Pacific, South Pacific Forum Working Paper No. 3, 1984.

West, F. J. *Political Advancement in the South Pacific: A Comparative Study of Colonial Practice in Fiji, Tahiti and America Samoa*. Melbourne: Oxford University Press, 1961.

3
Pacific Island Economies: Prospects For Development

As with developing countries elsewhere, the Pacific islands aspire to improve the living conditions of their peoples and to meet the challenges of the so-called revolution of rising expectations. Along with raising national income levels, they aspire to greater self-reliance, improved income distribution, and preservation of the natural environment. Yet, perhaps to a greater extent than developing countries in other regions, the Pacific islands are beset with powerful constraints to development—geographic, economic, and sociocultural constraints that can effectively frustrate the realization of development aspirations. This problem is particularly severe for the small islands.

This chapter focuses on the growth potential of the Pacific islands and on the principal constraints affecting their development prospects. It examines the economic structures of the island entities as well as the recent record in national income, foreign trade, and aid. It also discusses prospects for development, and concludes with an examination of several specific options that can promote future growth.

DEVELOPMENT CONSTRAINTS

The many geographic and physical disadvantages faced by the Pacific islands are familiar and have been enumerated in chapter 1. Two major characteristics are small physical size and remoteness from metropolitan countries. Except for Papua New Guinea, all the island entities have relatively small land areas (see table 1.1), although many have jurisdiction over vast EEZs. A corollary of small physical size is a narrow resource base that, in turn, restricts the range of development options. The resource base of the coral-based islands, such as Niue and Tokelau, is particularly circumscribed—many are essentially "resourceless rocks" characterized by the absence of such basic resources as rivers and streams, arable top soil, pastures and forests.

Environmental fragility is related to the special characteristic of smallness that requires great caution in island development efforts. Vital resources such as forests, water, soil, beach sands, reef, and lagoon areas can be quickly destroyed or seriously damaged unless proper environmental safeguards are implemented.

In addition to being remote from major metropolitan centers, the island entities are also separated by vast distances from each other. For those entities which themselves are spread over large areas of ocean, additional problems arise over the often high level of dispersion and the remoteness of outer islands from the main island. These physical characteristics exact a heavy economic burden: transportation costs are high, air and shipping services are infrequent and, in the cases of many of the outer islands, air service is often absent. The need to establish basic government, social, and economic services and facilities on outer islands also makes for high administrative costs.

Many Pacific islands are located in climatic zones that give rise to periodic natural disasters—hurricanes, floods, tidal waves, and drought. Because of their location, Fiji, Tonga, Guam, and the Northern Marianas are highly vulnerable to hurricanes that often inflict heavy damage on crops, dwellings, and infrastructure. Coral atolls are particularly vulnerable to tidal waves because of their low elevation, which also makes them the most vulnerable to rising ocean levels that have been predicted over the coming decades as a result of the global warming effects of damage to ozone layers.

Small domestic markets—tiny by world standards—are common, reflecting small populations and national incomes. An exception is Papua New Guinea with its population of 3.5 million, but even here national market size is effectively reduced by a market fragmentation due to poor transportation links—a problem that is also true of some of the other island countries. Small and often geographically dispersed populations combined with relatively low national income levels severely limit the potential for industrial diversification. Additionally, in the case of import substitution, opportunities to realize economies of scale are restricted.

As small, largely open economies, the Pacific islands are also exposed to the vagaries of world market forces and related influences that can significantly affect the level of economic activity.[1] Prices for exports can change sharply in the short term, and can remain depressed over an extended period. A heavy dependence on imported goods and services makes the islands vulnerable to imported inflation which can dis-

---

1 The manuscript for this book was completed before the conflict in the Persian Gulf in late 1990-91. However, the impact of rising oil prices and a decrease in tourist flows further underline the vulnerabilities of the island economies to events that are beyond the control of the island countries.

rupt domestic efforts to achieve price stability. Foreign aid and investment, frequently significant factors in the development of these countries, are by definition dominated by outside influences.

Shortages of basic factor inputs, particularly development capital and manpower skills, are additional constraints. Scarcity of capital funds is caused by low domestic savings reflecting such factors as low per capita incomes, weak personal savings habits, and undeveloped capital markets. A consequence of a weak domestic savings capacity is a high degree of dependence on foreign aid and private foreign investment.

Shortage of manpower skills often extends over a wide range—technical, professional, managerial, administrative, and entrepreneurial. Inadequate training in the past is largely responsible for present shortcomings but, in some cases, loss of skills through emigration has been important. The "skills gap" has been partly filled by the recruitment of expatriates, but this is a costly and not altogether satisfactory alternative.

Among such small economies scarcity of key skills can have a devastating effect on a particular economic sector if not on the economy as a whole. For example, the shortage of engineers can seriously obstruct the implementation of major infrastructure projects, while scarcity of entrepreneurs significantly undermines the growth of the private sector—potentially the most dynamic source of economic growth. The shortage of skills has broader implications as well; for example, it reduces a country's overall capacity to absorb and apply modern technical knowledge and ideas.

A further disadvantage faced by some Pacific island countries stems from inappropriate development structures and approaches inherited from the colonial past. Such structures, including government bureaucracies, business regulations, and planning systems, were often established in island countries without a realistic appreciation of local needs, administrative capacity, and resources. For these countries, the operation and maintenance requirements of such structures continue to impose a heavy financial burden with unfavorable consequences for development.

OTHER CHALLENGES

Cultural constraints can also seriously inhibit economic growth. Cultural influences reflect the fact that cultural factors and traditions are still powerful forces in contemporary Pacific island society. While the relationship between culture and economic development is not clearly understood, it is apparent that the continued existence of certain cultural institutions and practices has weakened the modernization process. Customary forms of land tenure, for example, can blunt incentives for agricultural production because a clear title to land is absent. Additionally, communal attitudes and related customary influences often clash with the requirements of a capitalistic- and individualistic-oriented economy, with adverse effects on economic efficiency and capital accumulation. Overcoming the negative effects of traditional culture so as to encourage economic growth will remain a major challenge.

As noted in chapter 1, almost all Pacific islands are experiencing rapid population growth. High rates of population growth can create many economic and social problems: a growing demand for jobs, pressure on social facilities and infrastructure, and a bias in favor of consumption as opposed to savings. Where emigration has been heavy, as in the Cook Islands and Niue, it has meant the loss of many people with skills and expertise who are needed at home.

These constraints underlie the basic argument often advanced that small Pacific islands should be treated as special development cases demanding new approaches and policies. However, the Pacific islands do possess certain advantages that can provide the basis for significant economic development. As noted by Hughes (1985:19), most are well endowed with agricultural land; the climate favors year-round cropping; the larger countries have minerals, forests, and hydroelectric power potential; and all have access to fisheries. South Pacific Forum island members enjoy special trade access to the markets of Australia or New Zealand, and in some cases there is special immigration for island workers. Moreover, the strategic value of the region is recognized, with implications for foreign aid. Also, in general the region is perceived as one of political stability where progress has been made in establishing basic infrastructure. Finally, the fact that most Pacific islands still have thriving subsistence sectors, complementing modern sector activity, is an additional positive factor.

That smallness and remoteness do not necessarily place absolute limits on economic development is also recognized. Smallness (especially if combined with compactness) can facilitate the spread of ideas and the fulfillment, nationally, of certain basic needs at modest cost. Small islands also have some potential to develop specialized income generating activities based on the exploitation of insularity and remoteness—for example, tropical plant research and export-oriented horticulture.

ECONOMIC STRUCTURES

The Pacific islands differ widely in physical size, population, and natural resources. Several, including Papua New Guinea, are relatively large and generously endowed with natural resources. Others, such as Kiribati and Tuvalu, have extremely small land areas and narrow resource bases. This often striking variation in resource endowment is closely reflected in the economic situation that has developed to date.

The economies of most Pacific islands are dominated by the primary sector—agriculture, forestry, and fisheries—inclusive of production that takes place in the non-monetary or subsistence sector. This dominance is particularly true of Cook Islands, Fiji, Solomon Islands, Tonga, Vanuatu, Western Samoa, and Papua New Guinea (despite the latter's substantial mineral production for export). Characteristically, primary sector production accounts for over half the total value of gross domestic product, and is even more dominant in terms of employment. In several of these countries, as much as 60 percent of the population is dependent on the primary sector for livelihood.

Primary sector activity in these countries contrasts strikingly with its role in several other Pacific islands, particularly the U.S.-associated entities such as the Northern Marianas, Guam, and even American Samoa (leaving aside fish processing based on catches by foreign vessels). Here, agricultural activity—both cash and subsistence—barely exists. This is due to such factors as rapid monetization of the economy (often artificially induced by foreign aid) and, in some cases, less than congenial agronomic conditions combined with official neglect. In Nauru, interest in agricultural production has declined over the years largely as a result of heavy concentration on phosphate mining.

Subsistence production continues to thrive, particularly in Solomon Islands, Papua New Guinea, Tonga, and Western Samoa, where characteristically it accounts for 25 to 30 percent of gross domestic product. Extensive involvement in subsistence activity gives rise to conditions of "subsistence affluence" in many areas, especially in the provision of foodstuffs, housing, and other basic needs for the indigenous population. It also provides an effective fallback when the monetary economy is depressed.

Mining is prominent in Papua New Guinea, especially of gold and copper, in New Caledonia, primarily of nickel, and, to a lesser extent, in Fiji and Solomon Islands. Nauru's almost complete dependence on phosphate mining has already been noted.

Papua New Guinea operates two of the largest mining complexes in the world: the copper mine in Panguna, Bougainville Island, which opened in 1972 (presently closed due to local turmoil), and the copper and gold mine at Ok Tedi in Mount Fabilan, in the Western Province, which opened in 1985. New Caledonia mines nickel from known reserves that, in size, are second only to those of Cuba, although in terms of present productive capacity it ranks third (along with Australia) to Canada and the Soviet Union. In both Papua New Guinea and New Caledonia earnings from mining dominate exports and play a prominent role in the national economies generally.

Manufacturing is widespread in the islands, especially for import substitution, but nowhere is it a major component of the economy except possibly in American Samoa with its substantial fish processing operations and Fiji with its garment industry. Not surprisingly, Fiji, Papua New Guinea, and New Caledonia exhibit the most diversified industrial sectors, characterized by several major processed products and a variety of import-substitute items. However, Tonga established a small Industries Centre in 1980, which has developed rapidly and now produces a variety of manufactured products for both the domestic and export markets.

In Fiji, major industrial products include sugar, garments, fish, coconut oil, concrete, cigarettes, beer, timber, wood products, biscuits, and corrugated iron roofing. Manufacturing activity associated with these and related items accounts for up to 12 percent of gross domestic product (GDP). In Papua New Guinea, industrial activity is dominated by export processing ventures, including sugar, palm oil, and wood products, combined with a wide range of basically import-replacement manufactures. For the smaller island groups (other than the smallest, which have virtually no industrial production), the characteristic pattern consists of one or two export processing ventures operating alongside a small number of basically import-substitution enterprises.

The service sector is significant in most Pacific islands. Government administration is usually dominant, but other significant sources are finance, tourism, and trading. This sector is particularly important in the small, resource-poor islands, accounting for at least 60 percent of GDP. In these cases, a government sector that has been inflated by foreign aid is sometimes combined with high levels of remittances from overseas kinsfolk and the development of philatelic services, tourism, and international finance centers.[2]

Foreign private capital has played a crucial part in developing many of the leading sectors noted above. This is understandable given the paucity of local capital funds and technical expertise throughout the region. Foreign investment inflows over time—largely through multinational channels—have resulted in foreign domination of key sectors of

---

[2] The term "MIRAB" has been coined (Watters and Bertram, 1985) to describe the economic structures of "transfer-service based" economies such as those of Cook Islands, Tuvalu, Niue, and Tokelau. MIRAB stands for *migration, remittances, aid, and bureaucracy,* which for these economies have, collectively, provided the main impetus for economic advancement—especially in terms of raising welfare levels.

many island countries, especially trading, mining, telecommunications, banking, insurance, and "up market" hotels (Fairbairn and Parry, 1986:2). Recent inflows of foreign direct investment have favored the natural resource sector, with a concentration on Papua New Guinea's mineral and petroleum exploration and mineral exploration in Solomon Islands and to a lesser extent in Fiji. In the Micronesian sub-region, the emphasis is on tourism development and fisheries projects in one or two cases. The sectors least affected by foreign investment are agriculture and small business.

NATIONAL INCOME

The coverage and reliability of national income statistics in the region vary, but based on the available data (see table 1.1), national per capita income levels are high by the standards of developing countries. National income per capita ranges from $430 to $12,800. Topping the list are Northern Mariana Islands, American Samoa, French Polynesia, Guam, New Caledonia, and Nauru—countries whose income levels have been boosted by special factors such as high levels of financial aid (including substantial budgetary assistance from metropolitan governments). In addition, American Samoa benefits from large-scale fish processing and personal remittances from relatives living abroad, Guam from the presence of a large military establishment plus tourism, and New Caledonia from nickel production and a large complement of highly paid expatriates including military personnel. French Polynesia benefits from tourism and a large military presence, and Nauru from phosphate mining.

Fiji's per capita income level—currently around $1,700—has been well above the regional average. This is the outcome of a generally sustained and fairly diversified growth pattern. The leading growth sectors have been tourism and manufacturing, supported by heavy foreign investment and by sugar and other natural resources. More recently Fiji has benefited from a dramatic growth in the garments industry. At the opposite end of the scale are Kiribati, Tokelau, Tuvalu, and Western Samoa, whose per capita incomes vary from $410 to $680; several of these countries receive large amounts of foreign aid, without which their income levels would be much lower.

Growth in the GDP appears to have been achieved by a few island states, although the performance of many cannot be judged due to lack of data. Fiji, Papua New Guinea, Solomon Islands, and Tonga show a consistent pattern of annual growth from the mid-1970s to 1985, although (except for Tonga) each experienced negative growth in at least one year during the 1981–82 world recession. For the period 1972–85, the annual percentage growth rate of real GDP according to Asian Development Bank (ADB) estimates averaged 4 for Fiji, 1.7 for Papua New Guinea, 7.7 for Solomon Islands, and 7.5 for Tonga (ADB, 1986:7). After accounting for population growth, these rates imply an increase in levels of real income per capita, with the exception of Papua New Guinea whose population grew by an average of 2 percent per year.

In the absence of detailed data little can be said about the trend in real national income of other island countries. The recent decline—at least up to 1986—in the price of major exports such as copra has meant that the trend in national income has probably been static or even negative. The available evidence for Cook Islands indicates a sizable decline during the 1970s, while the national income of Kiribati fell sharply in 1979 with the cessation of phosphate mining on Ocean Island.

FOREIGN TRADE

The relatively undeveloped nature of Pacific island economies is reflected in their export patterns. For the region as a whole, the most important natural resource exports are mineral products—principally nickel, gold, copper, and phosphate (see table 3.1). Next in importance are agriculture-based products, including sugar, palm oil, coconut oil, fruit and vegetables, cocoa and coffee, and processed fish and timber.

Manufacturing exports are significant in the case of Fiji where garments are now a leading industry, but the export of clothing from Tonga (mainly knitwear and leather jackets) and coconut cream from Western Samoa are also noteworthy.

The Pacific islands differ widely in the extent to which they have been able to diversify exports. Papua New Guinea can boast over a dozen major export items including coffee, cocoa, tea, copra oil, palm oil, gold, copper, silver, and forest products (see table 3.1). Fiji's exports are dominated by sugar, but several other products, including gold and timber, provide some diversification; Solomon Islands has at least five major export items including palm oil, logs, and fish. Among the smaller islands, traditional export products like copra and other coconut products are prominent and are often combined with various other natural resource and agricultural products. In several cases, a single product is of overriding importance, for example, phosphate in Nauru, nickel in New Caledonia, and canned fish in American Samoa.

Trade flows have been heavily influenced by the special ties that many islands have developed with metropolitan countries—largely reflecting political and historical associations—as well as by geographical and transportation factors. Major trading partners are the European Community (EC) countries (particularly France and the United Kingdom), Japan, the United States, Australia, and New Zealand. On the export

Table 3.1. Pacific Island Economies: Domestic Exports by Value and Principal Products, 1988

Country	Total exports (US$million)	Principal products
American Samoa	200[a]	Canned fish and other fish products
Cook Islands	4	Fresh fruit and vegetables, pearl shells, clothing, copra
Federated States of Micronesia	—	Copra
Fiji	304	Sugar, garments, gold, coconut oil, molasses, fish, timber products
French Polynesia	20[b]	Coconut oil, culture pearls, fruit
Guam	39[c]	Transhipped goods
Kiribati	5	Copra, fish
Nauru	116[d]	Phosphate
New Caledonia	202[e]	Nickel ore, non-ferrous metals
Niue	(0.08[a])	Coconut cream, lime
Northern Mariana Islands	4[a]	Vegetables
Palau	—	Copra
Papua New Guinea	1,409	Gold, copper concentrates, coffee, cocoa, forest products, palm oil, coconut products
Solomon Islands	77	Copra, canned fish, forest products, palm oil, cocoa
Tokelau	—	Copra, handicrafts
Tonga	8	Vanilla, coconut oil, clothing, watermelons, squash
Tuvalu	(0.7[c])	Copra, handicrafts, fish
Vanuatu	15	Copra, beef products, cocoa, logs
Wallis and Futuna	—	Trochus
Western Samoa	14	Taro, coconut oil, coconut cream, cocoa, timber

— not available
[a] 1985
[b] 1987
[c] 1983
[d] 1982–83
[e] 1984

Sources: Australian National University (1990), Asian Development Bank (1987), South Pacific Commission (1985), Carter (1984), Bank of Papua New Guinea (1987). Exports from Marshall Islands are not known.

side, there are many instances of an unusually heavy trade flow from one island to one or two metropolitan destinations, such as from American Samoa to the United States, from Cook Islands to New Zealand, and from French Polynesia to France. The same pattern is also apparent for imports as, for example, the flows from France to New Caledonia, from Australia to Papua New Guinea, and from New Zealand to Cook Islands.

With one or two exceptions, the export performance of the Pacific islands in recent years has been disappointing, and, in some cases, export volumes have fallen drastically. This situation, combined with low commodity prices in international markets at least up to 1985, has often caused serious balance of payments problems. In some countries, a large part of the deficit in the commodity accounts has been offset by personal remittances sent by overseas relatives and by foreign aid and related transfers. When transfers have not been sufficient to significantly reduce the pressure on the balance of payments, governments have resorted to a variety of corrective measures, including currency devaluation and foreign exchange control, tight monetary policies and reduction in public expenditures. Where these measures have been severe, a sizable contraction in the level of economic activity has often resulted. Current world prices for many of the region's major exports, such as coconut products, coffee, and cocoa, remain low so that for many Pacific island countries the balance of payments will remain under pressure. In large measure, the balance of payments of these countries have been underwritten by foreign aid, and if for some reason such aid were to decline, the adjustment measures that will have to be made will be socially and politically painful.

FOREIGN AID

For almost all Pacific islands, foreign aid has played a vital role in meeting government budgetary and development needs and in providing foreign exchange. Official development assistance (ODA), both bilateral and multilateral, flowing into the region is estimated at $1,176 million (1988—excluding the U.S.-associated Pacific islands) or approximately $230 per capita (see table 3.2). This makes the Pacific region one of the most heavily assisted regions in the world. These figures bespeak conditions of high aid dependency and reflect the essentially narrow revenue bases and saving capacity of individual countries. Narrow revenue bases reflect, in turn, low levels of per capita incomes, small modern industrial sectors, and deficiencies in tax collection systems.

Approximately 90 percent of official aid is bilateral, with Australia, France, and the United States the leading donors (Fairbairn, 1985a:67).

Table 3.2. Aid Flows to the South Pacific, 1988

Country	Total aid flows (US$million)	Aid per capita (US$)
Cook Islands	11	631
Fiji	43	58
French Polynesia	327	1,715
Kiribati	12	176
Nauru*	NA	—
New Caledonia	261	1,653
Niue	5	1,626
Papua New Guinea	300	84
Solomon Islands	35	117
Tokelau	3	1,446
Tonga	13	128
Tuvalu	13	1,585
Vanuatu	29	195
Western Samoa	19	113
Unallocated	55	—
Total	1,176	232

* Although aid figures for Nauru are not available, such aid would be negligible.
NA Not Available
— Not Applicable
Note: Aid flows (mostly in the form of budgetary assistance) to other Pacific island countries come to an estimated $300 million (see table 1.1).
Sources: Australian National University (1990: 37) and Fairbairn (1985a).

Aid from these countries is mainly budgetary assistance to former colonies or dependent territories. This is most evident in French and U.S. aid, which is heavily concentrated on those islands with which they have historic ties. By comparison, aid from Australia, New Zealand, and the United Kingdom is more widely dispersed among all the island countries (although the bulk of Australian aid goes to its former dependency, Papua New Guinea).

Aid from multilateral agencies is dominated by the European Community (EC) (under the Lomé Convention—an economic assistance arrangement with the Pacific islands and other former colonies), UN Development Program (UNDP), and several international financial institutions, such as Asian Development Bank (ADB) and the World Bank. Such aid is generally accorded to members of these organizations and, in some cases (e.g., ADB), mostly takes the form of soft-term concessionary loans. Technical assistance is prominent in the aid rendered by some multilateral agencies.

Major aid recipients are French Polynesia, New Caledonia, Papua New Guinea, and the U.S.-associated Pacific islands. Except for Papua

New Guinea and more recently the Federated States of Micronesia, the Marshall Islands, and the Northern Mariana Islands, these recipients are dependent territories, and usually the aid rendered is predominantly budgetary. The ranking alters somewhat when aid is considered on a per capita basis; among the leading recipients under this measure are the very small entities such as Cook Islands, Niue, Tokelau, and Wallis and Futuna.

High aid dependency is now a fact of life for all but a few island groups. Typically, ODA accounts for at least 40 percent of total government revenue—considerably more in some cases (e.g., Cook Islands and Western Samoa)—and between 35 and 50 percent of total government expenditure, both recurrent and development.

Such a heavy aid dependency can significantly affect the level of economic activity in the recipient country and cause major changes in economic structures. It can lead to excessively large public sectors which can give rise to serious inefficiencies in resource use (e.g., by crowding out the private sector). It can also make for an overvalued currency that weakens export activity and encourages imports. Other possible consequences include: lessened self-reliance, inflationary pressures, artificially high consumption demand, and exposure to political pressures from donors. However, despite these factors, support for foreign aid remains strong since it is recognized that without this assistance, meaningful development programs could not be sustained. For the sake of pursuing their growth objectives, most island leaders are prepared to accept, at least up to a point, the perceived negatives of foreign aid.

The future trend of aid to the Pacific island countries is now somewhat clouded due to recent international developments. These include the focus given to Eastern Europe by the industrial countries in terms of aid and capital flows. Reduced superpower rivalry in the South Pacific region might also, paradoxically, result in some reduction of strategically or politically inspired flows of aid into the region.

Prospects are that aid flows at current levels will continue; they may even rise substantially as new sources of aid open up. France, the United States, and Japan in particular have scaled up their assistance or are in the process of doing so, and are seeking to identify appropriate channels for increased aid. Recent evidence suggests that these donors are prepared to make substantial commitments over the long term. An example is the proposed U.S. government aid arrangement negotiated with Palau under the Compact of Free Association. This arrangement involves the payment of approximately $420 million in congressional appropriations and grants over a 15-year period. This includes $70 million to be set aside as a trust fund which is expected to earn an estimated $1.4 billion over a 50-year period.

Aid dependency therefore seems likely to remain high in the foreseeable future. Papua New Guinea, where budgetary aid from Australia is being progressively reduced, may be an exception although project aid grants from Australia are likely to increase substantially.

CURRENT DEVELOPMENTS

Almost all Pacific islands prepare formal development plans to assist in setting directions and mobilizing resources for their economic development. The nature and scope of these plan documents differ widely, but there are also many common elements. These elements include a statement of national development objectives that typically relates to the need to raise living standards and to achieve greater national self-reliance through a more intensive utilization of available natural resources. The plans also lay down various policies and strategies deemed essential for realizing declared development objectives, as well as detailed sectoral programs and projects for implementation during the plan period.

The development strategies of many Pacific islands—particularly the larger ones—emphasize the need to encourage foreign direct investment. This emphasis stems from the large capital requirements of technologically complex projects, such as in mining and other natural resource fields. As small developing economies, the islands simply do not have the wherewithal to develop such projects on their own. As a result, almost all the island entities have put in place tax incentive schemes, often quite generous, as well as other forms of assistance directed at encouraging foreign investment. Variously incorporated in special legislation or administrative guidelines and rules, these benefits typically include tax holiday periods, tariff and customs duty concessions, accelerated depreciation of plant and capital equipment and carry-over of financial losses. Direct forms of assistance often include the provision of fully serviced factory sites and subsidies for technical training.

Agriculture

Agriculture is almost everywhere accorded overriding importance in the islands' development programs. The main exceptions are the small atoll economies that lack suitable land for major agricultural expansion. The objectives in agriculture are to exploit land resources more intensively as a means of boosting local food supplies (and thus self-sufficiency) and strengthening export capabilities.

The physical and geographic circumstances of the individual island groups largely dictate the kind of agricultural program that is designed and implemented. The range of options is greatest among the larger islands. In Papua New Guinea, recent efforts have been devoted to the production of export crops, such as cocoa, tea, sugar, and palm oil, which have met with considerable success. Solomon Islands has developed palm oil on a large scale and experimented (unsuccessfully) with rice cultivation. In addition to sugar, Fiji has further diversified with cocoa, ginger, and fruit juices.

The smaller economies have little scope for embarking on major agricultural development and for reducing their already heavy dependence on imported foodstuffs. Nonetheless, they continue to emphasize maintaining levels of copra exports—usually the only cash crop of any importance—and strengthening subsistence production.

The severity of the agricultural problems of many Pacific island countries is demonstrated by the fact that production of major export crops, such as copra, cocoa, coffee, and bananas, has been declining. Low commodity prices in world markets have played a part in undermining production incentives. In addition, there are powerful constraints on the supply side. Copra, for example, has suffered from a failure to replace aging trees, and banana production has been affected by damage caused by pests and plant diseases. Small land areas, poor management, vulnerability to natural disasters, and problems over access to land controlled by customary forms of tenure are other serious impediments. These fundamental problems are not easily resolved.

Fisheries

As in agriculture, all the Pacific island entities are active in the exploitation of fishery resources for both domestic consumption and export purposes. Fisheries resources are particularly large where island countries, such as Fiji and Solomon Islands, have extensive EEZs that are well stocked with tuna. Fishing for local consumption, which generally takes place around coastal waters, is small in scale and is oriented toward both subsistence and local commercial needs. Export fisheries, principally for tuna, are carried out mainly in pelagic waters, using large-scale capital-intensive techniques. For many islands, coastal fisheries have limited potential, mainly because extensive shelf areas are lacking, but these fisheries will continue to be important, nevertheless, as a local source of food. The major potential for economic expansion is found in larger commercial operations in the islands' EEZs.

The region's tuna resources are harvested mainly by technologically advanced fishing fleets based in Japan, the Philippines, South Korea, Taiwan, and the United States. Total annual catch is estimated at 100,000 tons—equal to around one-third of the world tuna catch—which, unprocessed, is valued at around $55 million (Morrison, 1987). Approximately 80 percent of this catch is processed within the region, mainly in American Samoa.

Although the global tuna market has been depressed during the 1980s, the Pacific islands have benefited from recent developments in the tuna industry. These include (1) the movement of traditional fishing grounds from the eastern Pacific to the central and western Pacific, (2) the closure of tuna processing plants in the United States because of high operating costs, and (3) the trend toward the basing of purse seine tuna activities in the Pacific islands region to improve operational efficiency (Morrison, 1987).

Many islands have established shore-based tuna facilities, which sometimes have resulted in substantial financial benefits for the host country. Processing facilities for the production of canned tuna for export are located in American Samoa, Fiji, and Solomon Islands. These have a combined capacity of 160,000 tons, of which 140,000 tons are produced by the two canneries in American Samoa. The foreign tuna fleets maintain bases in at least 12 countries, while transshipment facilities exist in Palau and Vanuatu. Smoked tuna is processed for the Japanese market on a small scale in the Marshall Islands and Solomon Islands. Many of the island groups benefit from license fees (usually no more than 5 percent of the value of the catch) paid by foreign vessels for access to their EEZs over a specified time.

The island governments are seeking to further develop their commercial fishing industries, especially by increasing processing activities, and to gain greater benefits for themselves. Lacking the necessary technical expertise and capital funds, they have relied heavily on outside assistance via both bilateral and multilateral organizations. At the regional level, two organizations have been particularly active—the Forum Fisheries Agency (FFA) and the South Pacific Commission (SPC). The former has played a vital role in coordinating the economic and financial aspects of the industry while the latter has helped to establish the potential of tuna in the region through extensive survey work on stocks and migratory movement patterns.[3]

Forestry

The Melanesian islands, particularly Papua New Guinea, Solomon Islands, and Fiji, have extensive forest areas that have generated sizable export production. The main hardwood species are "Spanish" mahogany and sierra walnut, although large Caribbean pine plantations are found in Fiji. Forestry products, mainly logs but also timber, plywood, and woodchips, account for about one-sixth of the region's

---

[3] Additionally, the FFA represented the island states in negotiating a Fisheries Access Treaty between the U.S. government and 16 Pacific island countries that allows island members to benefit from U.S. fishing activities on their EEZs (See page 160).

total export earnings, with Papua New Guinea and Solomon Islands being the dominant exporters. Exports of non-coniferous saw and veneer logs from these two countries alone are responsible for up to 4 percent of world exports of these products (Morrison, 1987). Most large-scale export-oriented operations are owned by foreign corporations, principally Japanese.

In Fiji, substantial past investment in pine growing is beginning to pay off with the initiation of milling. In time this industry will make a significant impact on exports and on domestic timber supply and will stimulate other wood-based activities. Many industrial possibilities for Fiji pine have been identified for future development.

Several other Pacific islands have extensive forestry resources. Exploitation in these cases has been directed mainly at supplying local markets; only Western Samoa and Vanuatu have been able to produce for export, and these only in a small way. (The very small island countries do not have significant forests.)

A major problem facing the forestry sector is unregulated and extensive logging practices, which threaten to undermine the sustainability of forests as a natural resource. Many islands lack proper land-use schemes for deforested areas. Logging has led to serious soil erosion on deforested areas, and often also to extensive damage to catchment areas, rivers, and streams (Morrison, 1987). However, to date these practices seem to have attracted little concerted attention at the official level.

Minerals

As already noted, the Melanesian islands, which are extensions of mountain ranges of the Asian continent, are particularly well endowed with minerals. Several mining operations in the region are among the largest in the world and dominate the local economy to an unusual degree as, for example, the mining of copper and gold by two companies (Bougainville Copper and Ok Tedi) in Papua New Guinea (see page 43).

Much recent interest has centered on the mineral resources—copper, silver, plutonium, titanium, and particularly gold—associated with the so-called Rim of Fire. This zone represents the boundary of major Pacific tectonic plates that extend from the Philippines and Indonesia to Papua New Guinea, Vanuatu, Solomon Islands, Fiji, and south to New Zealand. The presence of minerals in this zone is due to volcanic and related actions caused by pressure associated with the movement of the tectonic plates. The mineral potential of the Rim of Fire is being actively explored. Prospects for the larger countries are very promising, and it is believed that some of the smaller islands located along this zone could also have significant deposits.

Exciting gold discoveries have recently been made in various locations in Papua New Guinea and several other islands, which when fully developed will place the Pacific region alongside South Africa and the Soviet Union as the world's leading gold producers. In Papua New Guinea, new gold deposits have been found in the central highlands and the small island of Lihir (Morrison, 1987). Potentially valuable deposits have been uncovered on Babelthuap in Palau, and new reserves have been identified in Fiji. Prospects for major gold discoveries in Vanuatu and Solomon Islands are promising.

Other mineral deposits have been found in the islands but for various reasons have not thus far reached the production stage. These include natural gas and oil in Papua New Guinea, copper in Fiji and Vanuatu, silver in Vanuatu, coal in Papua New Guinea, bauxite in Fiji and Solomon Islands, lead and iron phosphate in Fiji, and chromite sands in several island countries.

Extensive interest has also been shown in the potential for exploiting sea-based minerals in the region. These include manganese nodules, polymetallic sulfides on ocean sea floors, and cobalt-rich manganese on crusts of seamounts. However, with the possible exception of manganese, explorations to date have not identified significant deposits of these minerals within the maritime jurisdictions of these countries.

Other Possibilities

Except for the extremely remote islands, all the Pacific islands have some tourist potential based on natural beauty, cultures, and lifestyles—and even their relative isolation. Tourism remains a key economic sector in Fiji (although it suffered a temporary setback as a result of the military coups of 1987), French Polynesia, Guam, and the Northern Mariana Islands. Tourism is being actively developed in Western Samoa, Cook Islands, and several other countries. Its value as a foreign exchange earner is recognized, as well as its capacity to generate local economic growth and employment and to stimulate activity in complementary sectors such as construction and transportation.

Despite tourism's economic potential, a few of the island governments have chosen to limit the rate of development in order to reduce the impact on the local societies and cultures. In other cases, such as Papua New Guinea, growth has been impeded by a low priority accorded tourism in development plans relative to other options.

Foreign exchange earnings from tourism can be high as a proportion of total export values. In Fiji, gross foreign exchange earnings from tourism now exceed those from sugar, and in Western Samoa such earnings are nearly equal to total export earnings. (However, these findings may exaggerate the importance of tourism, particularly if foreign exchange "leakages" from these earnings have not been adequately taken into account.)

Scope for major expansion in tourism in the immediate future exists in the majority of the Pacific islands. However, achieving this expansion requires overcoming several major constraints, including problems in air transportation and poor tourist infrastructure. Action is needed to strengthen accommodation and recreational facilities, undertake promotional measures, and stimulate productive activities that support tourism. In certain cases, further development awaits changes in official attitudes.

Faced with many disadvantages, such as small and often highly fragmented domestic markets and capital shortages, the Pacific islands have not been able to carry industrialization very far. Such industrial development[4] as has occurred is dominated by a few export-oriented, agro-based ventures connected with sugar, palm oil, and fish and coconut oil. However, Fiji's garment manufacturing from imported cloth is a leading export activity, along with smaller manufactured products geared to both the domestic and overseas markets. The widest range of manufactures comprises import substitutes, particularly those that enjoy a natural advantage due to high transportation and related costs. Soft drinks, biscuits, concrete products, toilet paper, ice cream, and confectionary products are widely available. The fabrication of a range of clothing products for export based on imported raw materials is particularly important for Tonga and Fiji.

Active efforts are underway to exploit other industrial possibilities, particularly the processing of major natural resources. Industrial concessions, including tax holidays and tariff assistance combined with many forms of direct assistance, are available in most countries to stimulate industrialization. Complementing these measures are two special schemes provided by the governments of New Zealand and Australia, respectively—the Pacific Islands Industrial Development Scheme (PIIDS) and the Joint Venture Scheme.

For large investors, the most attractive opportunities at present are in minerals and hotels where large-scale investment projects can be developed. This has been the basic pattern to date, as evidenced by the foreign direct investment flows into Papua New Guinea and, to a lesser extent, Fiji and Solomon Islands. However, opportunities for foreign investment in other sectors can also be attractive, as is shown by Tonga's experience in small-scale industrial enterprises.

---

4 This is particularly true of import substitution; diseconomies of scale make it uneconomic to produce the range of goods that can be provided by larger countries (Tsusaka, 1984:67).

The range of development activities based on the exploitation of the extensive sea spaces (EEZs) under the jurisdiction of Pacific island countries can also be important. Opportunities in fisheries and in deep-sea mining have been noted above. However other possibilities include: energy from wave action and temperature variation, mariculture, pearl culture, commercial recreational activities, and ornamental shell materials. These possibilities may be particulartly important for the very small island countries with large sea-land ratios.

REGIONAL INITIATIVES

Regional cooperation at the intergovernmental level has been an important facet of Pacific islands development. The leading regional organizations and arrangements are discussed in chapter 4, but several initiatives concerning the trade, fisheries, and infrastructure fields should be mentioned here since they bear directly on the region's capacity to realize its productive potential.

In trade, a major initiative was taken in 1982 with the coming into effect of a regional trade and economic cooperation agreement between Australia and New Zealand and island members of the South Pacific Forum. (Papua New Guinea has a separate parallel agreement with Australia.) Known as the South Pacific Regional Trade and Economic Cooperation Agreement, or SPARTECA, this arrangement is designed to achieve progressively free market access for island exports into these metropolitan markets in order to stimulate economic development of the islands. Based on the principle of non-reciprocal preferential access in favor of island members, SPARTECA also commits Australia and New Zealand to cooperate in the development of the participating island members through non-trade channels such as joint venture arrangements, market promotion, and training.

Reviewed annually by a committee of trade officials from participant islands, SPARTECA has succeeded in considerably improving access for island products to the two metropolitan markets. Quota and tariff restrictions now apply to only three groups of products of interest to island members—garments, textiles, and footwear—but even here, restrictions have been applied minimally so that, in fact, there is virtually free access. New Zealand removed all trade restrictions in 1988 and Australia is committed to doing so (through a phasing-down process) by 1996; thus, problems over access have been largely resolved.[5]

---

5 In the case of Australia, trade restrictions will continue to apply to steel and motor vehicles—products of no real interest to island countries—and sugar, which is an item subject to general prohibition.

Improved access conditions have been of greatest benefit to Fiji and Tonga. Fiji has been able to increase the export of garments and timber products, while Tonga has had similar experience with a range of manufactured products, including woolen knitwear. On the other hand, for many of the small Forum island members SPARTECA has to date been of little value mainly because of supply limitations. The value of the trade concessions that Forum island countries enjoy under SPARTECA—and the Lomé Convention for that matter—is likely to decline over time given current worldwide trends toward trade liberalization. The challenge is therefore for Pacific island countries to become more competitive internationally and, particularly for the larger countries, to look for markets beyond Australia and New Zealand.

In fisheries, a noteworthy milestone was the negotiation of a Fisheries Access Treaty between the U.S. government and a group of 16 Pacific members, including Australia and New Zealand. Efforts are now being made to negotiate a similar region-wide fishing agreement with Japan. The treaty with the United States was an important achievement for the Pacific islands because it provides a framework for ensuring that the islands get financial benefits from the exploitation of their fisheries zones by the U.S. fishing fleet (organized in the American Tunaboat Association). Past poaching on the part of U.S. fishing vessels had caused much controversy and resentment against the United States on the part of island governments and the general public.

The treaty provides for the payment of $60 million in cash and in kind to the Pacific island states over a period of five years. Approximately one-sixth of this money consists of license fees and funds for technical assistance paid directly by the U.S. fishing industry; the balance is paid by the U.S. government, partly as assistance to the island fishing industry. The financial arrangements should help accelerate fisheries development in the islands.

In industrial development, island members of the South Pacific Forum have established manufacturing and agricultural industries under the auspices of New Zealand's Pacific Island Industrial Development Scheme (PIIDS). This program was introduced in 1976 to foster economic development and employment growth by assisting New Zealand entrepreneurs to set up manufacturing and processing operations in the islands. PIIDS encourages joint ventures with local businesses, with the New Zealand partner expected to own not less than 20 percent of the shareholdings. Through PIIDS, the New Zealand government provides a package of financial incentives to encourage the transfer of capital, entrepreneurial skills, and technology from New Zealand to the islands in accordance with the development goals of the host country. The New Zealand government meets part of the establishment costs and provides interest-free suspensory loans (up to a limit) that convert to a grant after five years of operation.

PIIDS has been instrumental in establishing over 40 businesses in the islands. Leading hosts are Fiji and Western Samoa, each with 11 PIIDS-assisted ventures, followed by Cook Islands and Tonga, each with 8 ventures. Approximately 1,200 jobs have been generated directly by PIIDS—a result that has been achieved with the expenditure of only a modest NZ $3.0 million (approximately $1.7 million) by the New Zealand government.

Australia has also established a scheme designed to promote investment in the productive sector of Forum island members. Through Australia's Joint Venture Scheme, financial assistance is provided to island governments to help fund island equity shares in ventures with Australian partners. Additionally, Australian government grants are available through this program to Australian businesses for feasibility studies on possible investment projects.

GROWTH PROSPECTS

The capacity of Pacific island economies to achieve sustainable growth appears to be closely related to their resource endowments—both sea and land-based—and to the presence of special factors that can sometimes compensate for paucity of resources. It also depends on the ability to exploit these resources through the implementation of sound economic policies and access to the finance and technical skills necessary for development. Favorable markets are also essential in the case of exports.

On the policy front, appropriate development policies must be designed and implemented to strengthen productive capacity. Among other things, such policies call for action to encourage private sector investment, promote increased savings, strengthen infrastructure, improve labor productivity, and stimulate export activity. Similarly, sound macroeconomic policies and national economic management are essential for establishing a favorable economic environment for long-term growth. The necessary policies call for appropriate fiscal, monetary, and exchange rate measures to contain inflation, prevent unsustainable deficits in the balance of payments and the public sector, and avoid excessive foreign debts. A major macroeconomic policy requirement is also to place greater reliance on market forces as a means of achieving greater efficiency in the allocation and utilization of resources.

The larger islands—the "group one" islands identified earlier comprising Papua New Guinea, Fiji, New Caledonia, and Solomon Islands—are the lucky ones of the region. Because of their substantial resource bases, each country has the potential to achieve long-term self-sustaining growth. Much progress has already been made in developing their resources and, as noted previously, the momentum continues in mining, forestry, agriculture, and associated processing activities.

Future success for the larger islands depends largely on improving existing knowledge about their resource potential and mobilizing the necessary capital and technical inputs. The amount of equity and technical knowledge required for development is often substantial and beyond domestic capacities; therefore, much depends on the ability to tap international markets, both official and private. An essential ingredient is the creation of a congenial domestic environment for investment and related entrepreneurial activities. This requires appropriate taxation regimes, investment guidelines, social and economic infrastructure, training and, most importantly, political and social stability. With these ingredients and favorable trading conditions, continuing economic growth and its corollary of rising living standards can be expected with a fair degree of certainty.

For the smaller island groups, economic prospects are far less bright. The middle-level island groups, such as Western Samoa and Tonga, and the tiny entities such as Kiribati, Tuvalu, and Tokelau, are the real problem economies of the region. They are bedeviled by narrow resource bases, geographic isolation, rigid land-tenure systems, and low capacities to save and innovate. The overriding constraint is simply an inadequate resource base to sustain economic growth over the long term.

The development predicament of these small islands has many symptoms: unusually high aid dependency, overseas migration, heavy dependence on imported foodstuffs and other raw materials, and, for some, a heavy reliance on personal remittances from overseas.

Dependence on foreign aid, overseas migration, and personal remittances will remain the major "options" for countering the disadvantages associated with limited development potential. These options are, in some cases, being combined with other initiatives including special employment schemes with international shipping and fishing companies and, in the case of Palau and Tuvalu, the establishment of trust funds by donors.

However, the economic and social costs associated with these approaches can be heavy and may even exceed the apparent benefits. As previously noted, foreign aid can seriously undermine national (and individual) initiative and can have serious distorting effects on the economy that undermine the efficient allocation and utilization of scarce resources. Overseas migration leads to the loss of talented people with technical skills and experience, while special employment schemes have the disadvantage that they can always be withdrawn at the whim of the sponsoring organization or country.

Small islands need to examine closely other possible strategies, particularly those that diminish the degree of their vulnerability to external forces. One possibility is the revitalization of subsistence activities as a complement to the monetary economy. Such a strategy requires a recognition of the development potential of the subsistence sector that, in some cases, has declined to the point of being barely visible, as well as the designing of appropriate policies to foster development. This approach also calls for renewed efforts to promote the adoption of appropriate technologies aimed at increasing productivity and for improving communications and transportation facilities for rural subsistence-based communities. A viable subsistence sector can help reduce dependence on imported foodstuffs, enhance self-reliance, and provide a measure of security against the instabilities of external markets.

Another course of action that merits more serious consideration is a concerted program of population control. The aim of population control is to reduce population growth, through a lowering of birth rates, to levels that the economy can reasonably absorb. Several islands have, in the past, launched population control programs with some success. But in general this is a matter which so far has received little serious attention. Where population densities are already high and emigration outlets non-existent, population control is imperative if subsistence poverty is to be averted or at least alleviated.

Finally, the forging of closer relationships with larger countries and international groupings outside the South Pacific deserves attention. This option applies to both large and small Pacific islands and has two aspects that are not mutually exclusive. The first aspect is the fostering, as a matter of deliberate policy, of closer integration with metropolitan countries (e.g., Australia, France, the United States, and New Zealand), which have or have had traditional links with the South Pacific islands. Closer integration can be attained by developing special economic relationships, such as preferential trading arrangements and common currency systems, or through constitutional and political change; for island countries, such integration can mean a more predictable basis for securing aid, trade, and emigration concessions. However, close integration with metropolitan countries can lead to erosion of national identity and cultural integrity—and ultimately political sovereignty—and therefore, Pacific island countries are unlikely to view this possibility as a feasible option.

A second possibility is for the islands to participate more actively in

Asia-Pacific regional cooperation, working with such regional arrangements as the Association of Southeast Asian Nations (ASEAN) and the Asia-Pacific Economic Cooperation initiative (APEC). Opportunities for promoting closer cooperation within the wider Asia-Pacific region will be discussed in chapter 5; but it can be noted here that so far the Pacific islands have had minimal involvement in these wider regional initiatives. The countries of ASEAN are part of the dynamic East Asian regional economy that is experiencing unequalled economic growth and rapid socioeconomic structural change. Closer cooperation with these countries and associated regional groupings could offer trade, aid, and training opportunities for the Pacific islands. Similarly, active participation in the APEC process would, among other things, gain a wider regional audience for island interests and development opportunities.

CONCLUSION

The Pacific islands face many difficult development problems—physical, human, and economic. Yet island countries have made substantial progress in building up productive capacity and setting the stage for further advances. Successes have been achieved in agriculture, mining, service industries and, especially for the larger countries, manufacturing and processing activities. In these endeavors, the islands have drawn heavily on the international community for financial and technical support as well as on their own regional institutions for technical assistance.

The capacity to achieve sustainable growth differs widely among the islands and is closely related to basic resource endowments. The best prospects are for the larger islands, especially Papua New Guinea, Solomon Islands, Fiji, and New Caledonia, where agriculture, fisheries, forestry, and minerals provide attractive development options. Here the challenge is essentially to put in place appropriate development policies and to mobilize the financial, human, and technical resources needed for development.

For the small islands, paucity of natural resources combined with other disadvantages almost assures "no growth" scenarios. The pressure of ever-rising populations on weak economic bases can be eased somewhat by taking advantage of various special opportunities, such as overseas employment schemes, cooperative arrangements with development organizations and countries within the broader Asia-Pacific region, and, over time, by encouraging population control. However, the economic consequences of restricted resource bases are almost inescapable. High-aid dependency will continue, as will pressures for emigration, while in the face of so many uncertainties and unknowns, the margins between adequate conditions of life and bare subsistence poverty will remain very thin. The plight of these small countries is a challenge both to their own governments and to the broader regional and international community.

REFERENCES AND SUGGESTED READING

Asian Development Bank. *Key Indicators of Developing Member Countries of ADB*, Vol. XVII (July), Manila, 1986.

Asian Development Bank. *Key Indicators of Developing Member Countries of ADB*, Vol. XVIII, Manila, 1987.

Australian National University. *Pacific Economic Bulletin*, Vol. 5, No. 1 (June 1988), National Centre for Development Studies, Canberra, ACT

Australian National University. *Pacific Economic Bulletin*, Vol. 5, No. 1 (June 1990), National Centre for Development Studies, Canberra, ACT

Bank of Papua New Guinea. *Quarterly Economic Bulletin*, Vol. XV, No. 4 (December 1987 Issue), Port Moresby.

Carter, J. *Pacific Islands Year Book*, 15th Edition, Pacific Publication, Sydney, 1984.

Castle, L.V. "The Economic Context" in Asian Development Bank, *South Pacific Agricultural Survey: Pacific Agricultural Choices and Constraints* (provisional printing), Manila, 1979, pp. 101–128.

Fairbairn, Te'o I.J. *Island Economies: Studies from the South Pacific*, University of the South Pacific, Institute of Pacific Studies, Suva, 1985a.

Fairbairn, Te'o I.J. and K. Kakazu. "Trade and Diversification in Small Island Economies with Particular Emphasis on the South Pacific," *Singapore Economic Review*, Vol. 30, No. 2, Singapore, 1985b, pp. 17–35.

Fairbairn, Te'o I.J. and T.T.G. Parry. *Multinational Enterprises in the Developing South Pacific Region* (Research Report Series No.1), Pacific Islands Development Program, East-West Center, Honolulu, 1986.

Hughes, H. "Asian and Pacific Developing Economies: Performance and Issues," *Asian Development Review*, Vol. 3, No. 1, Asian Development Bank, Manila, 1985.

International Monetary Fund. *International Financial Statistics*, Vol. XLI, No. 9, (September 1988), Washington, D.C.

Morrison, Charles E., editor. *Asia-Pacific Report: Trends, Issues, Challenges 1987–88*. Chapter 5: "The New Pacific Island States," East-West Center, Honolulu, pp. 57–70.

Siwatibau, S. "The South Pacific Countries and Regionalism," unpublished paper presented at the East-West Center Symposium on Cooperation in Asia and the Pacific, East-West Center, Honolulu, 1990.

South Pacific Commission. *Overseas Trade 1983*, Statistical Bulletin No. 27, Noumea, 1985.

South Pacific Commission. *South Pacific Economies 1985: Statistical Summary*, (pre-published draft), Noumea, circa 1988.

Tisdell, C.A. and Te'o I.J. Fairbairn. "Subsistence Economies and Unsustainable Development and Trade: Some Simple Theory," *The Journal of Development Studies*, Vol. 20, No. 2, Frank Cass and Co. Ltd., London, 1984.

Tsusaka, A. "South Pacific Developing Countries: Development Issues and Challenges," *Asian Development Review*, Vol. 2, No. 1, Asian Development Bank, Manila, 1984, pp. 65-81.

Wace, N. "Exploitation of the Advantages of Remoteness and Isolation in the Economic Development of Pacific Islands," in Shand, R.S. (ed.), *The Island States of the Pacific and Indian Oceans: Anatomy of Development*, Mono. No. 23, Development Studies Centre, ANU, Canberra ACT, 1980.

Watters, R.F. and A. Bertram. Comments in unpublished summary record of workshop on the subject of *New Zealand and Its Small Island Neighbours*, Institute of Policy Studies, Victoria University of Wellington, New Zealand, May 1985.

World Bank. *The World Bank Atlas 1987*, Washington D.C., 1987.

4
Regional Cooperation*

Regionalism has been a major and pervasive force in the Pacific islands' development. The establishment, in 1947, of the South Pacific Commission (SPC) by the six metropolitan powers with territorial interests in the region at the time—the United Kingdom, the United States, France, the Netherlands, Australia, and New Zealand—marked the beginning of regional cooperation at the intergovernmental level, although Pacific islanders played no part in this initiative.[1] Significant advances occurred in regional cooperation in the late 1960s and the 1970s, spurred on the one hand by the quickening pace of decolonization, and on the other hand by a growing consciousness among Pacific island leaders of a regional identity and common interests. Leading initiatives were the establishment of the South Pacific Forum in 1971, the South Pacific Bureau of Economic Cooperation or SPEC (now the South Pacific Forum Secretariat) in 1973,[2] and several specialized institutions in the field of higher education, shipping, trade, fisheries, and the environment. Also significant was the emergence—during the early 1980s—of a reconstituted SPC, through a series of measures converting it from a colonial body to one dominated by the Pacific islanders.

The proliferation of regional (and subregional) organizations and arrangements in recent years has meant that regional cooperation now touches practically every sphere of development in the region. Intergovernmental organizations, led by the South Pacific Forum, the Forum Secretariat, SPC, and the University of the South Pacific (USP),

---

* In preparing this chapter, the author relied heavily on the works of Neemia (1986); Fry (1979); and Crocombe (1981, 1983); he also benefited from contributions by Herr (1985); Kiste (1988); Axline (1984); and Baker (1985).

1 The Netherlands withdrew from the SPC in 1962 when it ceased to administer what was then Dutch New Guinea, now Irian Jaya under Indonesian rule.

2 At the 19th annual meeting of the South Pacific Forum, held in Nuku'alofa, Tonga, in September 1988, Forum members chose to rename SPEC as the South Pacific Forum Secretariat. For purposes of the present discussion, the latter organization will be referred to as the Forum Secretariat.

are active in major segments of the economic, social, and diplomatic-political life of the region, while cooperation within the private sector—which involves well over 200 separate arrangements—covers not only socioeconomic areas, but also religion, culture, and business. These institutions differ widely in their objectives, functions, organizational structures, funding arrangements, linkages with each other, and memberships. (One noteworthy feature of the leading intergovernmental organizations is the participation of metropolitan countries, like Australia, France, and New Zealand, either as members, donors, or both.[3])

This chapter highlights the main characteristics of regional cooperation in the Pacific island region, particularly in the economic area.[4] The discussion focuses on the main intergovernmental regional organizations—their organizational structure, objectives, functions, and role in the overall scheme of Pacific regionalism. It describes the basic nature and style of Pacific island regionalism, constraining influences, areas of conflict, and future prospects.

THE REGIONAL CONTEXT

South Pacific regionalism has been defined by a former secretary-general of the SPC, E.M. Salato, as "unity in diversity." Yet despite this diversity there is a pervasive sense of unity that is based on a whole nexus of common traditions, interests, and viewpoints. The fact that all are small, remote, resource-poor (except Papua New Guinea), and economically underdeveloped provides a common perspective as well as common problems in areas such as transportation, communications, education, and limited economic capacity. A Christian heritage, experience of colonial rule (except for Tonga which, nevertheless was a British protectorate during 1900-70), and the sharing of the resources of a common ocean have also been unifying elements.

Another unifying element in Pacific island regionalism has been "the Pacific Way," reflecting a non-confrontational consensual style of conducting discussions and arriving at decisions. The concept has also come to signify a common concern for the social and economic

---

3 The inclusion of Australia and New Zealand in the "metropolitan" group is somewhat misleading as it fails to recognize their unique position within the South Pacific regional schema; unlike the other metropolitans, Australia and New Zealand are members of the South Pacific Forum; are geographically contiguous; are recognized to have "special interests" in the region; and particularly in New Zealand's case, have developed a national image that reflects a close identification with the Pacific islands.

4 The economic bias means that little or nothing is said about regional projects in the fields of telecommunications, culture, health, and related areas. Also not covered are a number of national institutions that service the wider region (e.g., the Telecommunications Training Centre based in Fiji).

well-being of all participant members—large and small.

Yet the difficulties of Pacific islands' regional cooperation should not be minimized. Diversity alone can be an obstacle—the vast expanse of the region and the numerous political entities with differing political status and aspirations for the future present problems. Feelings of economic vulnerability can also blunt the incentive for regional cooperation, favoring instead such alternative strategies as continuing linkages with metropolitan countries. These constraints place broad limits on the process of regional cooperation.

Regional cooperation in many other parts of the world has been motivated largely by security and political considerations. In Western Europe, for example, regional cooperation in the post–World War II period was prompted primarily by the desire to avoid future conflict among the states of that region—particularly in the event of a resurgence of Germany. The establishment of the Association of Southeast Asian Nations (ASEAN), too, reflected a desire to create a cooperative framework capable of maintaining peace among members and deterring outside threats. In both instances, cooperation in economic and social areas was viewed primarily as a means toward the attainment of political and security objectives.

Pacific island regionalism has stemmed from a different environment and set of motivations. The fundamental security issue for the islands has been and remains that of economic viability, and correspondingly the major threats are not disputes over borders and territory but dispersion, isolation, and the common lack of resources. Cooperation among the islands has had little to do with market-sharing approaches (e.g., free trade, customs union, development banking, industrial planning, and free factor movement) designed to promote integration. It has also eschewed cooperation specifically aimed at achieving some sort of political union or federation, although some such proposals have been made (Moore, 1982). Rather, cooperation is pursued by the islands primarily as a means of performing a variety of specific tasks that contribute toward national development goals and related objectives both among the members and in the international sphere.

Thus regionalism in the Pacific has concentrated on the vigorous pursuit of cooperation in a range of functional-technical and diplomatic fields, many of which are vital for the region's development. In these areas, Pacific regionalism is as advanced as that found in any other developing region.

Many of the benefits of regional cooperation for the islands are essentially a function of scale. As small, scattered entities, the Pacific islands lack the resources to provide the full range of services normally associated with nationhood. Regional cooperation offers these states the opportunity to share common services and facilities on a cost effective basis. Services that particularly lend themselves to cooperation for economies of scale include transportation and communications, education and training, research and information sharing. This approach is still more attractive when these services are underwritten by external donors and hence entail little direct cost to the member countries. This aspect of regional cooperation is particularly compelling for the smaller islands.

Regional cooperation has also been a valuable mechanism for the Pacific islands in the international-diplomatic arena. Pacific island entities share common diplomatic facilities which would be beyond the reach of individual countries. Examples are office facilities in New York used by several Pacific island members of the United Nations (funded by the Australian government), and common representation in Brussels for the Pacific island members of the African, Caribbean, and Pacific group (ACP) associated with the European Economic Community.

A collective approach in international dealings has substantive advantages for the islands as well. A common position in international forums strengthens the voice of the islands on issues affecting the development and security of the Pacific island region. Group representation also provides a stronger bargaining position in negotiations over practical issues such as trade, aid, resource exploitation, and related areas, and can win for the islands greater benefits than would have been possible had they negotiated individually. (Note, however, that in some instances the islands have also benefited from splits in their ranks that have enabled the group as a whole to exploit competition among those with whom they were negotiating.) Finally, regionalism has also assisted the Pacific islands in asserting their cultural and political identity in a wider world context.

REGIONAL ORGANIZATIONS

As indicated at the start of this chapter, regional cooperation in the Pacific now comprises an extensive, albeit somewhat loose, network of organizations and arrangements that cover many key areas of development. This is the product of an evolutionary process that began with the establishment of the SPC in 1947 under the aegis of the metropolitan powers, and was characterized by a heightened involvement of Pacific island leaders from the mid-1960s, leading to the establishment of the South Pacific Forum in 1971. The creation of the Forum, in turn, served as a catalyst for the extension of regional cooperation into key functional areas such as fisheries, trade, and transportation.

Fundamental to this process was the determination of Pacific island leaders to assert their own control over regional organizations and to develop arrangements that would meet the many new demands of nationhood. A major challenge in this respect was the decolonization of the SPC—a process that was not completed until the 1980s.

The regional constellation of organizations is dominated by the South Pacific Forum, supported by the Forum Secretariat. Other major organizations are the South Pacific Commission (SPC) and the University of the South Pacific (USP). The Forum's premier position derives from the fact that representation at its meetings is always at the top level of government, and its decisions thus carry the full weight of the governments represented. Various functional organizations have also been established in major areas of development, including fisheries, the environment, shipping, and offshore mineral exploration. The major regional organizations and arrangements are discussed below, beginning with the SPC.

The South Pacific Commission

As indicated at the start of this chapter, the SPC came into existence in 1947 with the signing of the Canberra Agreement by the six metropolitan powers with colonial interests in the region at the time. This initiative was inspired largely by Australia and New Zealand—influenced not only by the principles of the Atlantic Charter as it applied to colonial dependencies but also by security considerations including the prospect of a diminished role by the United Kingdom in Southeast Asia and the Pacific. As provided for in the preamble of the Canberra Agreement, the SPC's objective was to "...encourage and strengthen international cooperation in promoting the economic and social welfare and advancement of the peoples of the region." This objective, however, did not apply in the political sphere, in which the SPC was specifically excluded from playing an active role.

Up to the 1970s the SPC operated essentially as a colonial structure dominated by the metropolitan powers. It functioned as a consultative and advisory body to the metropolitan governments and not to the island territories themselves. Decision making was the prerogative of a board of commissioners from each metropolitan country—who were assisted in their work by a research council of technical specialists and a secretariat based in Noumea. Also provided for as a mechanism for assisting the commissioners was the South Pacific Conference—the first meeting of which was held in 1950—when representatives of the dependent territories could voice their views and express opinions on the SPC's work program.

Under constant pressure from the island representatives, particularly from the mid-1970s, the SPC has progressively shed its colonial trappings (see appendix 2). Through a series of reforms, control of SPC affairs has now passed to island members. The South Pacific Conference is now the permanent decision-making body, and all island countries, regardless of political status, are now full participating members with an equal voice and voting power in SPC proceedings.

The SPC is the most comprehensive of the region's intergovernmental organizations, with membership extending to all Pacific islands plus the five continuing metropolitan members. Its work program continues to focus on practical development and training work in fields such as agriculture, fisheries, rural employment promotion, health, education, and the collection and distribution of social and economic data. The major mission is to promote the social and economic well-being of island communities at the grass roots level.

Despite its colonial origins, the SPC has been a significant force in promoting regional cooperation and (not always deliberately) in shaping a regional identity. It continues to act as a major channel for dispensing multilateral aid in the region, with particular emphasis on the development needs of its small island members. Apart from the practical benefits flowing from its work program, the staging of the Pacific conferences has provided a valuable forum for island leaders to come together and to discuss wider regional issues. The SPC has also been directly responsible for spawning other regional initiatives. Examples are the South Pacific Games (first held in 1963), the Festival of Pacific Arts (1972), and the South Pacific Regional Environment Programme (SPREP).

Yet the SPC continues to attract controversy, suggesting that it still has not found its proper niche. It is believed in some quarters that the metropolitan members, who contribute the bulk of the SPC's funds, still dominate SPC affairs—often in subtle ways. Others argue that the SPC duplicates some of the work being done by other regional bodies—a view that helped kindle interest in amalgamating SPC and the Forum Secretariat to form a single regional organization (SRO). The SRO concept was studied for some years, and led to the establishment of the South Pacific Organizations Coordinating Committee (SPOCC) in 1988 to coordinate all regional organizations.

The South Pacific Forum

The South Pacific Forum was established in 1971 on the initiative of the five Pacific island countries which had attained independence or self-governing status—Cook Islands, Fiji, Nauru, Tonga, and Western Samoa. These countries were all associated with the British Commonwealth and for several years had cooperated as members of the Pacific Islands Producers Association (PIPA)—established in 1965 and concerned predominantly with the marketing of bananas in the New

Zealand market. PIPA (which was terminated in 1973 and its functions taken over by SPEC) can be regarded as the region's first indigenous intergovernmental organization.

The first meeting of the South Pacific Forum was held in Wellington, hosted by the New Zealand government, with both New Zealand and Australian representatives present as observers (both were admitted shortly thereafter as full members). The island leaders saw a clear need for such an organization—and had discussed the matter informally at South Pacific Conferences from 1967 to 1969 and at Fiji's independence celebrations in 1970. As they saw it, a new regional institution was needed to promote the wider interest of the region at the political level and to meet the challenges opened up by nationhood. Such an organization would provide a forum for open and free-ranging discussions on regional and international issues. The SPC could not meet these needs due to its exclusion of political debate, and its unwillingness at that time to respond to the islanders' demand for a larger voice in SPC affairs.

Membership of the South Pacific Forum has grown from the initial group of 5 to its current membership of 15, an enlargement reflecting the further political evolution of the island region.

The need for a "trade secretariat" to implement regional activities mandated by the Forum led to the establishment of the South Pacific Bureau of Economic Cooperation (SPEC) in 1973 (see appendix 2). As specified in the SPEC Agreement, SPEC's functions were "...to facilitate cooperation and consultation between members in trade, economic development, transport, tourism, and other related areas." In 1975, SPEC was given the added responsibility of providing secretariat functions for the Forum and in 1988 was renamed the Forum Secretariat. Based in Suva and headed by a secretary-general, the Forum Secretariat has a professional staff of around thirty.

Economic, political, and strategic issues have dominated Forum affairs. This emphasis was clear from the outset when Forum discussions gave prominence to such issues as trade, shipping, tourism, civil aviation, energy, foreign investment, and atmospheric tests of nuclear weapons in French Polynesia. Trade issues were a major focus in the early period: how to reduce trade barriers, the feasibility of an economic union, ways to increase intraregional trade, and possibilities for improved access to the markets of Australia and New Zealand.

More recently, political and strategic issues have assumed increasing importance. French nuclear testing in the region continues to preoccupy the Forum, but several other political issues have attracted attention, including the future political status of New Caledonia, the extra-constitutional change of government in Fiji, and the South Pacific Nuclear Free Zone Treaty.

Also at the forefront of recent Forum meetings have been matters relating to resource conservation and the environment, including attempts to ban drift-net fishing in the region and the use of Pacific islands as a dumping ground for nuclear and toxic wastes.

A major initiative taken under the auspices of the South Pacific Forum was the signing of a trade and economic cooperation agreement—the South Pacific Regional Trade and Economic Cooperation Agreement, or SPARTECA—between the Forum island members and Australia and New Zealand. Based on the principle of non-reciprocal preferential access for the products of the island members, SPARTECA provides a framework for progressively achieving free access into these two metropolitan markets for as wide a range of products as possible.

Other notable regional measures include the establishment of a shipping corporation—the Pacific Forum Line (PFL); a fisheries agency—the Forum Fisheries Agency (FFA); an environmental program organized jointly with SPC—the South Pacific Regional Environment Programme (SPREP); trade promotion offices overseas—the South Pacific Trade Commission in Sydney and the South Pacific Trade Office in Auckland; and support for an offshore minerals exploration body—the South Pacific Applied Geoscience Commission (SOPAC). (See appendix 2 for a summary description of these organizations.) These initiatives would have been unlikely without the South Pacific Forum.

On the political front, the South Pacific Forum has been active in articulating a regional position on regional concerns, for example opposing French nuclear testing in French Polynesia and supporting the re-inscription of New Caledonia on the list of the United Nations Decolonizing Committee. The South Pacific Nuclear Free Zone Treaty was another notable initiative.

The South Pacific Forum meets annually at the head-of-government level; special sessions have also been convened from time-to-time to deal with specific matters. Meetings are informal and self-regulating, there being no formal charter or rules to guide proceedings. It is a unique institution affording political leaders the opportunity to come together informally, to get to know one another, and to discuss matters of common interest frankly and at length. This attribute of the South Pacific Forum has been a major element in fostering regionalism, promoting a stable regional environment, and ensuring that the "Pacific Way"—decision making based on consensus and harmony—is more than just a fanciful notion.

Another significant initiative was taken in 1989—following the South Pacific Forum meeting in Tuvalu—in the form of Post-Forum Dialogue meetings, with major donor countries and organizations. Participating countries (leaving aside Australia and New Zealand) include the United

Kingdom, the United States, France, Japan, and Canada. The basic aim of the dialogue meetings is to strengthen links with major donor countries and to highlight the major development needs of the Forum island countries.

The University of the South Pacific (USP)

Regional cooperation in tertiary education began in 1967 with the establishment of the USP. As envisaged by Pacific island leaders at the time, this facility would play a vital role in meeting the manpower needs of the developing island entities and in allowing Pacific islanders to be trained in an island setting where problems of cultural alienation would be minimized. It would also play a part in fostering a regional spirit among future leaders.

With its main campus located in Suva, USP embraces 11 island members,[5] although the USP is now the major source of university education only for 3 of these. Papua New Guinea has developed its own university system, as have the French territories. The former U.S. territories north of the equator traditionally used the University of Guam, but now use a wider range of sources, including degree-level facilities within their own territories. There are today 10 degree-awarding universities in the Pacific islands, with a likelihood of 12 by the end of 1990 and 15 by the end of the century.

USP has four teaching schools: the School of National Resources, the School of Social and Economic Development, the School of Education, and the School of Agriculture. The latter school is located at Alafua, Western Samoa, on a site formerly occupied by the Western Samoa South Pacific Regional College of Tropical Agriculture.

Alongside the schools are seven action-oriented institutes and several research units.[6] The institutes were established in the late 1970s as vehicles for promoting development in the region through practical activities such as applied research, consultancy, advisory work, and short courses.

To more effectively serve the needs of its far-flung constituency and to project its regional nature, USP operates an Extension Service Unit,

---

5 The 11 members include all Forum members except Australia, New Zealand, the Federated States of Micronesia (FSM), and Marshall Islands. The latter 2 are applying for USP membership.

6 These institutes are the Institute of Research and Extension Training in Agriculture (IRETA), Institute of Rural Development (IRD), Institute of Education, Institute of Pacific Studies, Institute of Social and Administrative Studies (ISAS), Institute of Marine Resources, and Institute of Natural Resources. A Centre for Applied Studies in Development was also established, but this institution was recently terminated and its role taken over by the institutes.

controlling a network of extension centers operating in nine member countries. The unit focuses on the promotion of "distant education" away from the Suva campus, including adult education. Its teaching work is facilitated by the use of satellite communication, while the regional centers play an important role, not only in teaching students but also in fostering broader community awareness.

The regional flavor of the university is reflected in its governance. The ceremonial head of USP is the chancellor—presently the head of state of Western Samoa. (Previous heads were the king of Tonga, the president of Nauru, the governor-general of Solomon Islands, the president of Kiribati, and the prime minister of Fiji.) The governing body, the University Council, is composed of both university personnel and representatives from all member countries, Australia, New Zealand, and regional organizations such as the SPC. However, administrative and teaching staff are overwhelmingly from Fiji, largely owing to constraints imposed by the Fiji government on the employment of other islanders.

USP has been an ambitious regional venture with few precedents in other parts of the world. It has had its share of problems: shortage of development funds, inadequate physical facilities, high staff turnover, and controversy over Fiji's dominant presence. Many from the other islands continue to believe that USP, which has been the recipient of substantial outside aid, has benefited the host island disproportionately. This belief has been a factor in the establishment of the National University of Samoa and the planned establishment of national universities in Tonga and Solomon Islands. Recent political events in Fiji have posed additional problems. Despite these problems, however, USP's contribution to the region's development through teaching, training, and research work has been widely acclaimed. It has also served as a valuable means of fostering regional attitudes and consciousness.

Other Regional Arrangements

Two other intergovernmental organizations of interest are the Pacific Basin Development Council (PBDC) and the Pacific Islands Development Program (PIDP).

PBDC was established in 1980 as a forum for the governors of the three American territories—American Samoa, Guam, and the Commonwealth of the Northern Marianas—and the state of Hawaii to discuss common social and economic development concerns and to explore possibilities for joint action. Particular emphasis has so far been given to the development of natural resources such as fisheries, agriculture, and energy, as well as to possibilities for improving local infrastructure and services, including transportation. PBDC is a non-profit, public organization and is headquartered in Honolulu.

PIDP was established in 1980 at the East-West Center in Honolulu by Pacific island governments following a conference of island leaders on Pacific island development issues (see appendix 2). PIDP's research and training agenda, which is set by the Pacific island leaders, emphasizes policy-oriented work in priority development fields such as fisheries, indigenous business development, natural disaster response, and private sector development. All Pacific islands as well as interested metropolitan countries can participate in PIDP.

Characteristics of Regional Cooperation

Several characteristics of regional cooperation stand out. First is the preeminence of the South Pacific Forum network, with its involvement, through various agencies, in many key functional areas of development. This involvement also extends to several other regional schemes not touched upon in this text—for example, regional consultation in the fields of tourism, civil aviation, and business.

A second salient characteristic is the participation of metropolitan countries as active members of the leading regional organizations, notably the South Pacific Forum and the SPC. Membership of Australia and New Zealand in the Forum was by invitation, in recognition of geographic and regional realities; that of the five metropolitan powers in the SPC is based on historical circumstances. This participation of metropolitan powers in the Pacific islands' regional organizations contrasts with regional cooperation elsewhere, such as ASEAN and the Caribbean Community and Common Market (CARICOM), which typically excludes metropolitan membership.

Thirdly, Fiji's leadership role has been a conspicuous feature of Pacific regional cooperation. The leading regional personality for many years was Ratu Sir Kamisese K.T. Mara, Fiji's prime minister for all but a short interval since independence. Ratu Mara led the so-called Lae rebellion of 1965, when Pacific island representatives at the Sixth South Pacific Conference challenged the long-standing dominance of the metropolitan powers in the SPC. He was also a leading figure in founding PIPA, the South Pacific Forum, and PIDP. Additionally, Fiji's leadership role has been helped in some degree by its central location and its links with both Melanesia and Polynesia, which have made it popular as a base for many regional and international agencies.

Finally, South Pacific regional cooperation has been, and continues to be, heavily underwritten by metropolitan sources. Over the last few years as much as 97 percent of SPC's budget, both administrative and work program, has been funded by participating metropolitan governments and international organizations in accordance with an agreed formula. Two-thirds of the Forum Secretariat's recurrent budget is funded by Australia and New Zealand, and the remaining third is provided by island members in accordance with an agreed formula. (This arrangement also applies to FFA.) The Forum Secretariat also derives substantial extra-budgetary funds from metropolitan donors and international organizations. The bulk of USP's income comes from student fees and member government grants, but outside contributions, especially for capital works, are still significant. Without such support, regional cooperation would probably have taken place on a much more modest scale.

WEAKNESSES AND FAILURES

The Pacific islands have attempted to cooperate in other areas of development, but with limited success due to a variety of factors including a preference for limited forms of cooperation and disagreements over the distribution of benefits. Notable "failures" include proposals to establish a single regional airline, a regional development bank, and an economic union.

The concept of a single regional airline, as opposed to national air carriers, was advanced mainly by Fiji during the early 1970s. Such a regional line was to be based on an existing consortium (Air Pacific) in which Fiji was a major shareholder along with three international airline companies and in which several islands held small shareholdings. (One of the latter group, Western Samoa, was already operating its own national airline as well.) The proposal pointed to the advantages of a single airline, especially the cost savings stemming from a rationalization of operations and the spin-off effects on other sectors such as tourism.

Fiji's proposal for a single regional airline failed to win support from the other island members of the consortium. There was disagreement over the nature of the proposed venture, with some islands feeling that such a venture would benefit Fiji disproportionately. Lack of a firm commitment was also evident from those islands that had or were establishing their own national airlines.[7]

The possibility of establishing a regional financial institution— either a development bank or a development fund—was the subject of several studies during the 1970s. In light of the relatively undeveloped nature of national financial institutions at the time, the general shortage

---

7 With the rejection of a single air carrier, Pacific islands have chosen to cooperate in other ways in this field. Thus, an Association of South Pacific Airlines has been formed (1979), as well as a Regional Civil Aviation Council—both serviced by the Forum Secretariat. Also, the Forum Secretariat assists island members in improving national civil aviation facilities.

of capital funds, and the noted success of the Caribbean Development Bank, island leaders thought that a regional financial facility could play a valuable role, especially in providing venture capital for major productive projects. Such a facility was of particular interest to the small islands that either lacked a national development bank or were not affiliated with an international financial institution.

While the concept of a regional financial institution was well received by the smaller islands and was shown—at least on paper—to be technically feasible, it failed to materialize. The reasons for this throw additional light on the constraints on regionalism in the South Pacific. A major obstacle was the apparently large amount of capital that such an institution (especially a development bank) would require, combined with an apparent lack of interested donors. Another factor was a decision by the Asian Development Bank (ADB) to strengthen its lending activities in the region—a move that in the eyes of certain island countries weakened the case for a new financial facility in the region. (ADB has now established a regional office in Port Vila, Vanuatu.) An additional difficulty—one voiced more recently—was the feeling among some islands that further proliferation of regional organizations was not desirable.

The possibility of establishing an economic union among Forum island members was among the ideas considered by the South Pacific Forum at its first meetings. By fostering free trade and cooperation in related areas, it was argued that such a union would set the stage for economic growth through closer integration of the island members' economies. However, upon closer examination, it was decided that the concept was premature, given the economic circumstances and trading capabilities of island countries at the time. As a result, the Forum turned to other options for fostering economic cooperation, including the negotiation of trade preferences with Australia and New Zealand and a regional sugar agreement between Fiji (as a supplier) and several other Pacific island members.

THE FUTURE

Various future possibilities for regional cooperation in the economic sphere have been identified. Many of these, if implemented, would constitute moves toward higher forms of regional integration. Among these possibilities are the removal of intraregional trade barriers, harmonization of industrial tax incentives, promotion of industrial planning, coordination of fiscal, monetary, and trade policies, and research on root crops and other major agricultural products. Other possibilities are more intensive cooperation in tourism development, civil aviation, development finance, the strengthening of education and training facilities, and the exchange of technical information.

However, many of these proposals are of little more than academic interest given the current regional environment and attitudes. One factor is a widespread reluctance to carry the process of regional cooperation to the point where political sovereignty is significantly compromised. Concern over political sovereignty is understandable, especially as many islands have only recently won their independence and are still preoccupied with the basic tasks of nation building. Another reason for a lack of enthusiasm for new initiatives is that, in some cases, the benefits of regional cooperation are not clear-cut. For example, given the tiny and undiversified nature of Pacific island economies, the removal of trade barriers may have little positive impact in stimulating intraregional trade and enlarging product markets to the point where economies of scale can be realized.

Other constraints on further significant advances in regional economic cooperation are the broad limits imposed by the vastness of the region, the lack of political sovereignty of some desirable island participants, and a general wish on the part of island leaders to consolidate what has already been achieved and to assess the effectiveness of existing regional organizations. Also relevant are doubts over the fair distribution of benefits (and costs) of regional projects, the persistence of strong traditional links with metropolitan countries (particularly in aid, trade, and education), and the ever-present problem of finance.

Practical steps to extend regional cooperation in the anticipated future are more likely to be taken in the fields least affected by the national sovereignty issue and where the benefits are unambiguous. This category would include relatively non-controversial activities such as product research (especially root crops), harmonization of foreign investment policies, and aspects of responding to natural disasters. Additionally, regional cooperation can be extended in many established areas.

Progress can also be made subregionally—where two or more island entities enter into cooperative arrangements over particular areas, including some of the difficult ones noted above. The sugar agreements negotiated between Fiji and several other Pacific islands are an example in the trade field. Such arrangements, modest as they might seem, can be viewed as a "second-best" solution, but they could lead to the formation of broader regional groupings.

In the diplomatic-international arena, prospects are for a strengthening of regional cooperation as the region becomes increasingly drawn into the currents of global events. Many critical issues affecting the region's development and well-being can benefit from a regional response; examples are regional security, the environment, and economic imperatives such as trade, aid, and technical assistance. These issues, among others, will continue to challenge the South Pacific Forum in its role as the region's primary international mouthpiece.

The future pattern of regional cooperation—and even the pace of development itself—is also likely to be influenced by certain divisive forces apparent in Pacific regionalism. One such force that has recently emerged, particularly manifested in the affairs of the South Pacific Forum, is a Melanesian-Polynesian cleavage, based on differences in viewpoints and approaches as perceived by these major cultural-ethnic groups. Papua New Guinea, Solomon Islands, and Vanuatu have established a "Melanesian Spearhead Group" as a discussion group that usually meets prior to Forum meetings to examine issues of particular concern to Melanesians. The Kanaks of New Caledonia were admitted to the Spearhead Group in 1990. On the Polynesian side, the king of Tonga has encouraged the islands of Polynesia to cooperate more closely in the cultural sphere to make them more aware of their common heritage. The full implications of the formation of the Melanesian Spearhead Group are not clear, although on the basis of experience to date it does not seem to be a serious threat to broader regional cooperation and institutions.

Another source of tension in Pacific regionalism is a degree of cleavage between the large and small islands. Given differing resource endowments and development prospects, it is to be expected that the interests and viewpoints of these two groups of countries should, on certain issues, diverge. Small island groups tend to feel that the larger ones fail to appreciate the special problems of very small economies, and they resent the fact that the benefits of regional cooperation tend to accrue mostly to the larger islands.

Additional tensions arise from the heavy dependence on metropolitan funding sources and from overlap in the work of the two major regional institutions—South Pacific Forum Secretariat and the South Pacific Commission. On the first point, many island leaders are concerned that over-reliance on outside aid provides leverage for metropolitan countries, in particular, to exert undue influence on the region's development. These concerns have been borne out by various experiences.

Concerns over duplication in the work of the SPC and the Forum Secretariat have been long-standing and are particularly voiced by the Melanesian islands, especially Papua New Guinea and Vanuatu. These two have been highly critical of the SPC's separate existence. Such fears were an important stimulus to consideration of the possibility of merging the SPC and the Forum into a single body—a Single Regional Organization (SRO).

An additional complication in regional cooperation arises from Fiji's "traditional" leading role. Papua New Guinea sees itself as the more natural leader of the grouping. Fiji's claim to leadership has also been undermined by the perception that it has gained disproportionate benefit as the location of the headquarters of most regional bodies, and by the 1987 military coups.

CONCLUSION

Regional cooperation in the South Pacific is both extensive and seemingly robust. It has given rise to a system of regional (and subregional) institutions of which some are multipurpose in function and others mainly concerned with specific sectors of activity. Through these established institutions, led by the South Pacific Forum, the South Pacific Forum Secretariat, the South Pacific Commission, and the University of the South Pacific, a multiplicity of tasks is carried out in pursuit of the interests and aspirations of island members.

As in many other developing regions, cooperation in the Pacific has been functional in character and strongly motivated by development and diplomatic aspects. Particular emphasis has been given to the sharing of common services and the diplomatic representation on regional and international issues affecting the peace and stability of the region. Regional cooperation as a conscious means of attaining closer integration of the economic life of island countries has made little headway; nor has cooperation to promote political union.

The future direction of Pacific island regionalism remains uncertain. Much will depend on available opportunities, perceived benefits, and political will. Several new areas of possible cooperation, such as intraregional trade promotion and industrial planning, are particularly difficult areas for multinational cooperation, as they inherently impinge upon national sovereignty and as such may be unacceptable to some member countries. Heavy capital requirements for some ventures and the response of outside donors to requests for assistance are also relevant considerations. Additionally, the future patterns of development will likely be influenced by the intraregional rivalries and tensions that have surfaced in recent years. For these and related reasons, the further progress of Pacific island regionalism, at least in the foreseeable future, is likely to be somewhat halting—and certainly far less spectacular than in its early, formative period.

REFERENCES AND SUGGESTED READING

Axline, W.A. "South Pacific Region Cooperation in Comparative Perspective: An Analytical Framework," *Political Science*, Vol. 36, No. 2 (December, 1984), pp. 40–49.

Baker, R.W. *Asian-Pacific Regionalism: New Structures, Old Impulses*, Occasional paper of the East-West Center, Honolulu, 1985.

Crocombe, R.G. *Regional Cooperation Among Island States: A Comparison of the Pacific and the Caribbean*, unpublished manuscript, The University of the South Pacific/East-West Center, Suva/Honolulu, 1981.

Crocombe, R.G. "Regional Cooperation: Overcoming the Counter-pulls," in Crocombe, R.G., (editor) *Foreign Forces in Pacific Politics*, Institute of Pacific Studies, The University of the South Pacific, Suva, 1983.

Fairbairn, Te'o. "The Role of Regional Organizations in Development: the SPC and SPEC," in Fairbain, Te'o I.J., *Island Economies: Studies from the South Pacific*, Institute of Pacific Studies, The University of the South Pacific, Suva, 1985.

Fry, G.E. "Regionalism and International Politics of the South Pacific," *Pacific Affairs*, Vol. 54, No. 3, 1981, pp. 455–484.

Fry, G.E. *South Pacific Regionalism: The Development of a Indigenous Commitment*, unpublished thesis submitted for Master of Arts, Australian National University, Canberra, 1979.

Herr, H. *Regional Cooperation in the Pacific Islands*, Pacific Islands Development Program monograph, East-West Center, Honolulu, 1985.

Kiste, R.C. "Cooperative Regional Organizations of the South Pacific Islands," unpublished paper, Honolulu, 1988.

Moore, M. *A Pacific Parliament: A Political and Economic Community for the South Pacific*, Institute of Pacific Studies, The University of the South Pacific, Suva, 1982.

Neemia, U.F. *Cooperation and Conflict: Costs, Benefits, and National Investments in Pacific Regional Cooperation*, Institute of Pacific Studies, The University of the South Pacific, Suva, 1986.

Piddington, K. *South Pacific Forum: The First 15 Years*, South Pacific Economic Cooperation, Suva, 1986.

Salato, E.M. "Unity in Diversity," *South Pacific Bulletin* (4th Quarter) Sydney, 1976.

Smith, T.R. *South Pacific Commission: An Analysis After Twenty-five Years*. New Zealand Institute of International Affairs, Wellington, 1972.

5
The Islands and the World

INTRODUCTION

The Pacific island nations are new actors on the world stage. Prior to the 1970s, what international relations existed in the island region were those among the colonial powers. Only within the past decade and a half has the island region witnessed the establishment of a system of international relations in which the indigenous nations are significant and independent players. As this system has emerged, it has drawn new outside powers into regional politics, including China, Japan, and the Soviet Union. Australia, New Zealand, and the United States, which had long taken the Western orientation of the island region for granted, have had to readjust their policies toward the region. This chapter will explore the evolution of the foreign policies of the island nations, the interests of the outside powers, and the main issues that have arisen in the island nations' relations with the outside world.

THE FOREIGN POLICIES OF THE ISLAND NATIONS

The New Foreign Policy Activism

The Pacific island nations are in the process of developing independent foreign policies. When they first began to recover their independence, foreign policy was low on their list of priorities. For each, the principal foreign relationship remained with the former metropolitan country and for very practical reasons. With the partial exception of Vanuatu, all of the currently independent or freely associated states received their independence without revolution or serious opposition from their colonial authority. Their first generation of leaders had extensive firsthand contacts with the respective colonial powers, and maintained affinities with these countries. Moreover, the island countries were highly dependent for budgetary support and trade on the former administering countries. This is a major factor in reinforcing postcolonial relations with Australia, New Zealand, the United Kingdom, and the United States. In some cases extensive emigration to the metropolitan countries had taken place and continued; Niue and Cook Islands even preferred a continuing dependency status with New Zealand in order to maintain complete freedom of emigration, and freedom to travel to and from New Zealand.

Other practical considerations also discouraged early foreign policy activism. Maintaining embassies abroad is very costly for the extremely small island nations. This is one reason why four independent island nations—Kiribati, Nauru, Tonga, and Tuvalu—have chosen not even to seek United Nations membership. Also, few islanders had training appropriate to diplomatic work. The key priority for the island governments was and remains economic development, and thus their limited professional expertise understandably has been concentrated more directly on development programs.

Since the early 1980s, however, there has been greater attention in some of the island states to foreign policy. There are several reasons for this. One is the existence of issues of region-wide concern, such as fisheries, environmental concerns, and completion of the self-determination process. The South Pacific Forum provided a venue for island leaders to discuss these political and diplomatic questions. The Forum became a more energetic international actor, as a consequence of both increasing nationalism within the island region and more self-confidence by the island states in their ability to deal with the outside world.

By the 1980s, the larger Pacific islands—Papua New Guinea (PNG) and Fiji—had developed professional (though very small) foreign ministries staffed by their own citizens, and some diplomatic missions abroad. Moreover, a new generation of younger island leaders was emerging who were less attached to the former colonial countries and more disposed to foreign policy experimentation. Further, as more outside powers became interested in the island region, the island states were able to take advantage of this attention and competition to further build their own international contacts.

Three countries—PNG, Vanuatu, and Fiji—have had the most active foreign policies.

Papua New Guinea

The largest of the island nations, PNG has the widest set of international relationships. For PNG, the relationship with Australia has been paramount. At the time of independence in 1975 Australian aid accounted for approximately half of the PNG budget; twelve years later, it was still a quarter of the budget. In December 1987 the two countries signed an understanding on the principles of their relations, including a pledge to consult in the case of external aggression against PNG.

However, especially under the leadership of Paias Wingti, the country's prime minister between 1985 and 1988, PNG has sought to reduce the centrality of its tie with Australia by strengthening its relations with other countries. These efforts have most prominently included Indonesia, China, Japan, the United States, and more recently the USSR.

Wingti described the relationship with Indonesia as having priority in his country's foreign policy. The Indonesian-PNG relationship, however, has been a troubled one. The two nations share a long land and river border splitting the island of New Guinea between Indonesia's West Irian Province and PNG. Many Melanesians, in PNG and elsewhere, regard Indonesia as a "colonial" power ruling a subjugated Melanesian population. A small separatist group, the Free Papua Movement (OPM), operates in West Irian. Indonesia has suspected that the organization receives assistance from across the border, and at times Indonesian military forces have crossed the border in pursuit of the OPM or to attack villages and refugee camps on the PNG side of the border from which the OPM was believed to operate. Some 10,000 refugees crossed to the PNG side of the border in 1983-84 during one serious flare-up in this fighting.

Under Wingti's leadership, a Treaty of Mutual Trust, Friendship, and Cooperation was signed with Indonesia in 1986, and Wingti visited Jakarta in January 1988. The relationship still remains a very sensitive one, and the border incursions feed the suspicions of some in PNG that Indonesia has designs on the entire island.

A significant recent development in PNG foreign policy has been an effort, launched in March 1988, to develop the Melanesian Spearhead Group, with Solomon Islands and Vanuatu (and now with the Kanaks of New Caledonia as well), as an activist subregional grouping. The Spearhead agreement provides that the three countries will cooperate among themselves in the political, economic, social, and cultural fields and on foreign policy issues of mutual interest. Those who support the Spearhead movement maintain that the South Pacific Forum is not aggressive enough in promoting island causes. This development has created latent tensions with other Forum countries, because the Spearhead establishes, in effect, an activist caucus in an organization whose operating style has been based upon the accommodative "Pacific Way" of consultation and consensus. Moreover, the member countries of the Spearhead group appear to be preferring their Melanesian partners to other Pacific island states primarily because of ethnic affinities. Although those in the Spearhead movement maintain that this is not so and that their positions will benefit all the island countries, they find it difficult to convince those who are less attracted to the policy position adopted by the Spearhead group. Some analysts fear that the Spearhead movement might eventually cause open rifts within the Forum, or the establishment of a corresponding Polynesian group.

Vanuatu

Another Spearhead country, Vanuatu, has acquired a reputation as having the island region's most radical foreign policy. Vanuatu's path to independence was a difficult one. Under the New Hebrides condominium run by Great Britain and France, the independence movement had to overcome French opposition, and an abortive rebellion against the new government by separatist forces was suppressed only with the help of the army of Papua New Guinea. From the beginning, Vanuatu's political leaders were less attached to the previous colonial powers and more willing to develop an active and independent foreign policy.

As might be expected from its historical development, Vanuatu's foreign policy activism has been most prominent in relation to continuing decolonialization issues, especially the question of independence for neighboring New Caledonia. Under Prime Minister Walter H. Lini, an Anglican priest, Vanuatu proclaimed a policy of nonalignment; declared itself a non-nuclear zone; established diplomatic relations with the Soviet Union, Cuba, and Libya (although no resident embassies were established); and voted frequently for causes pushed by radical third world nations in international organizations. Some ni-Vanuatu have received military training in Libya although there is no evidence that they have been involved in terrorism. There were reports in 1986 and 1987 that Libya hoped to use its Vanuatu connection to provide military assistance and training in terrorism to leftist elements of the Kanak resistance in New Caledonia. The mainstream Kanak leaders, however, rejected Libyan assistance, and diplomatic pressures from Australia, New Zealand, and other Pacific island nations may have helped persuade Lini in May 1987 to cancel plans for the opening of a Libyan embassy in Port Vila that could have served as a base of support for such an operation.

Vanuatu's Libyan diplomacy reportedly owed much to a radical wing of the ruling Vanua'aku Party, led by party secretary-general and businessman Barak Sope. Sope also was a strong supporter of a pan-Melanesian federation. The political rift between Lini and Sope, sparked by Sope's attempt to replace Lini as prime minister after the November 1987 elections, and Sope's subsequent expulsion from the Vanua'aku Party, may result in a more moderate Vanuatu foreign policy, at least as long as Lini remains prime minister. Lini was partially disabled by a stroke suffered while visiting the United States in February 1987, but has remained politically astute and in control.

Fiji

The third main foreign policy actor in the Pacific islands, Fiji, dominated the movement toward regionalism during the late 1970s and into the 1980s. Under Prime Minister Ratu Sir Kamisese Mara, Fiji pursued a basically conservative foreign policy, maintaining close links with Australia, New Zealand, and the United Kingdom, while gradually developing ties with China, Japan, and the United States. With U.S. encouragement and financial support, a Fijian armed forces contingent has been part of the multinational force and observers in the Sinai; Fiji also contributes troops to the UN peacekeeping contingent in southern Lebanon.

Fiji's regional role, however, has declined, both because of the rising activism in Melanesia and as a consequence of the 1987 coups. The coups disrupted Fiji's links with Australia and New Zealand, and when, after the second coup, Fiji was excluded from the Commmonwealth, it was isolated from its traditional friends. This encouraged it, however, to further diversify its foreign relations. France, clearly hoping to benefit from Fiji's isolation, was the first donor country to provide new aid after the coups. Ties were also improved with Indonesia and Malaysia, both of which expressed empathy for the concept of the paramount rights of indigenous populations.

Regional Institutions

Despite the development of more independent and active foreign policies by PNG, Vanuatu, Fiji, and to a lesser extent by Solomon Islands and Tonga, most Pacific island countries find the financial and human resource costs of an activist foreign policy prohibitive. Partly for this reason, regional institutions play a much more important role in coordinating foreign relations than in any other region of the world. The South Pacific Forum is particularly significant in this context. It is through the Forum that the island members, with Australia and New Zealand, have developed positions on a nuclear-free zone and New Caledonia. Likewise, the Forum Fisheries Agency helped the islands negotiate a multilateral tuna agreement with the United States, a formula which may supplant bilateral negotiations with other major distant-water fishing nations. The relatively slow and moderating processes of developing consensus in the "Pacific Way" through the Forum are constraining for the more activist countries (one of the factors, for example, stimulating the establishment of the Melanesian Spearhead Group). Yet regional institutions are likely to continue to play a leading role in the foreign policy development of the island nations.

THE INTERESTS OF THE MAJOR POWERS
The United States, United Kingdom, Australia, and New Zealand

Island foreign policy development took place against a background of growing strategic competition in the region. Through most of the post–World War II period, the Pacific was an "ANZUS lake." The French and British presence in their own colonies and protectorates added to American, Australian, and New Zealand influence. Because of the lack of competitive outside interests, these countries could largely take for granted their continuing domination of the island region. Moreover, it was presumed that the island societies' religious, social, and political conservatism and close traditional relations with the metropolitan countries would be a deterrent to outside involvements, particularly with the Soviet Union. The U.S. approach during this period has been characterized as one of "benign neglect," concentrating on its own territories and deferring to its allies to maintain a presence and relationships with the other island entities.

This situation began to change in the mid-1970s when the Soviet Union first showed an interest in the island region, offering fisheries agreements and scientific cooperation. This forced the ANZUS nations to look more closely at their own objectives in the region (Dorrance, 1980). These were quite similar for the three ANZUS members as well as the United Kingdom. In their analysis, the island region had been a bastion of peace and stability because it was largely unaffected by large power rivalry. The Western allies believed that the introduction of Soviet influence challenged the relative tranquility of the region and required them to increase substantially their attention to and investment in the region's security in order to maintain "strategic denial" of this region to potential hostile forces.

As the regional leaders of Western policy, Australia and New Zealand maintained the widest-ranging economic and cultural linkages with the island states and also encouraged and participated in regional cooperation, especially through the South Pacific Forum. U.S. assistance and diplomatic representation were also (modestly) increased. (While British assistance continued at moderate levels, direct British involvement with the islands continued to decline as the last of the British dependencies achieved independence in 1980.) Regionalism played an important role in maintaining a basic consensus on regional issues and foreign policy behavior.

Australian, New Zealand, and American involvement in the region has continued to increase over the past decade. Three-quarters of New Zealand's development assistance goes to the region, and over half of Australia's. Both also now provide significant security assistance to the island states—for example, Australia is supplying maritime patrol craft to a number of the island countries. The United States has continued a gradual expansion of its economic assistance programs and disaster relief activities in the independent island states (plus large aid packages to the former Trust territories under the Compacts of Free Association), and has further increased its diplomatic presence in the islands. A first-ever summit meeting between the U.S. president and leaders of the 13 independent island states in Honolulu in October 1990 symbolized the increased U.S. attention to the islands and in the eyes of the island leaders helped replenish the "pool of goodwill" towards the United States that had begun to dry up during the period of benign neglect.

Although the three ANZUS states share many common interests and objectives in the island region, their individual interests differ in important ways. There has long been economic competition between Australia and New Zealand in the region, as well as differing views as to which has the deeper ties and better understanding of the islands. Similarly, although both of the antipodean states have encouraged greater U.S. attention to the region, they also share a degree of apprehension that the United States may act in an ignorant and heavyhanded way—and may not heed their advice.

The United States has taken different positions from its ANZUS partners on several key regional issues. As a nuclear power which conducted tests in the region, and a supporter of the French nuclear capability and testing, the United States is an object of regional anti-nuclear concerns. Australia and New Zealand support island efforts to restrict nuclear activity in the region. Specific differences over the South Pacific Nuclear Free Zone Treaty are described in the following section. (New Zealand's adoption in 1984 of a ban on port access by nuclear-powered or armed ships led to the suspension of U.S. military cooperation and, in 1986, the formal suspension of the U.S. security commitment to New Zealand under ANZUS.) U.S. non-recognition of coastal state jurisdiction over migratory fish species created serious frictions with the islands over this major economic issue (also discussed further below), while Australia and New Zealand accept island jurisdiction and have assisted the islands in building their surveillance and enforcement capabilities.

Australian and New Zealand relations with the islands have their own sensitivities. As developed states and former colonial powers, their position within the South Pacific Forum grouping is somewhat ambivalent, and energetic advocacy by them of proposals can generate resistance and suspicion. They have taken different positions from the islands on some political issues, such as the 1987 Fiji coups that Australia and New Zealand criticized far more strongly than any of the other Forum members. Economic relations with Australia and New Zealand are much more important for the islands than for the two larger countries, both of whose trade remains overwhelmingly oriented toward other advanced states with membership in the Organization of Economic Cooperation and Development (OECD). And finally, there are also social-ethnic issues. New Zealand has significant islander communities, but there is some sensitivity between New Zealand's Maoris and islanders over competition for jobs and government funds. Australia could be a major safety valve for island population pressures, but it is difficult for islanders to qualify under the skill and family reunion criteria of Australia's current immigration system, and immigration levels from the islands remain very low.

There are differences between the Australian and New Zealand perspectives as well. New Zealand views itself as a Pacific nation and sees the island region as its primary area of geographic and security interest. For Australia, Asia has always been and remains the primary focus of security policy. Australia also disagrees with New Zealand's ban on nuclear ship visits and, while continuing security cooperation with New Zealand in the region, gives higher priority to its broader ANZUS links with the United States.

As the international contacts and politics of the island states become more varied and complex, the regional approaches of the ANZUS states seem likely also to continue to become more multidimensional and differentiated.

France

France shares the basic strategic interest of the other traditional colonial powers in the region: to prevent the intrusion of outside countries that might introduce more radical politics to the island region. However, French colonial policy, with its heavy emphasis on diffusing French culture and its strong resistance to decolonization, has perhaps been the chief force in introducing radical politics into the region. French resistance to Vanuatu's independence has been described, and French policy toward New Caledonia pushed the New Caledonian independence movement in a militant direction and, for a time, appeared to be giving the Libyans an opportunity to intervene in the region. France's strategic interest in the nuclear testing facility at Mururoa in French Polynesia has reinforced its reluctance to consider greater autonomy for this territory.

France's troubled relations with the independent island states over these issues and nuclear testing, however, have resulted in recent active French attempts to win over the island governments with offers of aid and enhanced cultural and political relations. As pointed out above, after the 1987 coups in Fiji, France moved quickly to improve its own relations with that important island nation. France also was among the first donor states to respond to various natural disasters in the islands during this period. At a meeting in Noumea in early 1989, French civilian and military officials responsible for the South Pacific formally adopted three priority policy objectives: increased contacts between the French territories and the island countries; closer involvement of the territories in the making and conduct of French policy in the region; and intensified French relations with the regional states and organizations. French efforts in this regard have focused particularly on the smaller Polynesian island groups such as Cook Islands, Tonga, and Western Samoa.

China and Japan

China and Japan have both historical associations and new ties with the Pacific island nations. Chinese immigrants in the 19th century worked on plantations or became small businessmen around the region, although the current Chinese population is not large. Japan acquired the German colonies in Micronesia as a League of Nations mandate after World War I and occupied other territories during World War II.

The recent diplomacy of the two countries toward the region reflects their own aspirations as Asia-Pacific powers and in part their concern about Soviet interests in the region. China has also engaged in a diplomatic rivalry with Taiwan, which maintains diplomatic relations with Solomon Islands and Tonga. Taiwan aid projects in the region have included funding for a new medical complex in Solomon Islands and an agricultural mission in the Marshall Islands. Taiwan's fishing fleet also has been active in the region, sometimes leading to frictions with the island governments. The People's Republic of China (PRC), for its part, has gained diplomatic footholds in the region by establishing embassies in Fiji, Papua New Guinea, and Western Samoa. Beijing's attention to the region was indicated by then-party leader Hu Yaobang's visit to those three countries in connection with his trip to Oceania in 1985. A Federated States of Micronesia (FSM) delegation headed by former President Tosiwo Nakayama visited Beijing in 1987, followed by a business delegation from the Marshall Islands. PRC oceanographic research vessels also have made port calls in Micronesia, reflecting China's increasingly active maritime posture in the Pacific Ocean.

The Japanese are becoming a much more important force in the islands. Japan has been the major fishing power in the region and imports timber and minerals. Japanese tourist investments are growing, and private interests are stimulated by prewar and wartime associations.

For example, a large foundation established by politician and gambling magnate, Ryoichi Sasakawa, who had spent some time in the islands during the war, hosted 10 island leaders at a conference in Japan in August 1988 and has established a $100 million fund to assist economic development in the region.

Japanese government policy in part reflects the desire of its leadership "to share international responsibilities" with the United States and other Western nations. When questions of potential political instability and Soviet involvement in the region arose in the mid-1980s, it seemed to Japan's foreign ministry that this was an area where Japan's economic strength and low-key political approach might help shore up Western influence. A decision in 1986 to increase economic assistance reflected Japanese concern over declines in Australian and British aid in the region and the Soviet-Kiribati fishing agreement. In January 1987, Foreign Minister Tadashi Kuranari visited several island nations in the region, announcing new Japanese aid plans and telling an audience in Suva that Japan "cannot support the introduction of new tension into this peaceful and untroubled region."

The Soviet Union

Soviet interest in the region was first displayed in 1976 when the USSR approached Tonga requesting a fishing agreement and shore rights. Tonga ultimately declined to deal with the Soviet Union, but the demonstration of Soviet interest resulted in a dramatic increase in Australian and New Zealand aid. Soviet activity in the island region, however, continued. Moscow reportedly sought to influence labor unions and interfered in the 1982 Fijian elections. Overtures were made for collaborative maritime research and fishing agreements. These efforts were all unsuccessful until 1985 when the Soviet Union concluded its first fishing agreement in the region, with Kiribati, as discussed below. Another fishing agreement was concluded in early 1987 with Vanuatu.

A clear formal indication of increasing Soviet interest in the islands was inclusion in then General-Secretary Mikhail Gorbachev's major statement on Soviet Asia-Pacific policy in Vladivostok in July of 1986 of a specific reference to Soviet desire for improved relations with the island nations. The USSR welcomed the South Pacific Nuclear Free Zone Treaty and quickly acceded to its protocols relating to the nuclear powers. Other themes in Soviet diplomacy in the region included criticism of ANZUS, French policy in New Caledonia, and U.S. policy in Micronesia. Soviet visits to the islands increased, and by the end of 1990 the Soviet Union had established its first resident embassy in the region in Papua New Guinea.

The Soviet Union does have scientific and fishing interests in the

Pacific Ocean. However, Western analysts have generally ascribed increased Soviet diplomatic activity in the island region to political objectives—"fishing for more than fish" in the expression of former U.S. Pacific Commander-in-Chief Ronald Hays. As a global power, the Soviet Union wants to have a presence and, if possible, some real influence in a region from which it has been hitherto virtually excluded. By taking strong, positive stances on the nuclear-free zone and New Caledonia, issues problematic for the United States, the Soviet Union hopes to gain popularity with the island governments. The Soviet Union has also had military objectives in the region; at the least its fishing fleet serves intelligence functions, while increased access to the island region might also help enhance Soviet knowledge of the geography of the Pacific Ocean, improving its ability to carry out anti-submarine warfare.

The general reorientation of Soviet policy under Gorbachev toward reduced East-West competition and an emphasis on domestic reform has at a minimum even further reduced the resources available for what was already a low-priority area of Soviet policy, and has almost certainly reduced the strategic element in this policy. Nevertheless, the Soviet Union clearly will maintain its broad objectives of greater acceptance and involvement in the Asia-Pacific region generally, and this will include continued efforts to normalize and broaden its contacts with the island states.

REGIONAL ISSUES

For the Pacific islands as a group, the most important issues and the greatest source of contention in their relations with outside nations fall under three headings: fisheries—their most important common economic resource; environmental questions including nuclear testing, waste disposal, and the fundamental threat of the greenhouse effect; and decolonization. In all three areas the island countries have carried out energetic, coordinated international efforts to advance their interests.

Fisheries

Fisheries have provided the most contentious single issue to date in U.S. relations with the island region. Fisheries also gave the Soviet Union its first real entree into the region, and figure importantly in island relations with other major Asia-Pacific actors including Japan, Korea, and Taiwan.

The 1982 UN Convention on the Law of the Sea, although not yet fully ratified, in practice confirmed claims by coastal states to a 200-mile Exclusive Economic Zone (EEZ). Negotiation of the treaty prompted all of the island nations and dependencies to declare EEZs between 1977 and 1984. Especially for the land resource-poor countries in

Polynesia and Micronesia, the new zones promise significantly enhanced resources from their vast surrounding seas. The most immediate of these is a share of the revenues derived by foreign fishing fleets, principally those from Japan, Taiwan, South Korea, and the United States. Along with the question of exploiting this resource, legal control has also confronted the islands with the issue of how to manage and conserve the resource.

Following the completion of the UN Convention, Japan, Taiwan, and South Korea basically accepted the jurisdictional claims of the islands and negotiated access agreements according to which they paid licensing fees. The United States, however, refused to recognize the jurisdiction of the islands within these zones over "highly migratory" fish species (i.e., tuna, the main fishery resource of most of the islands).

The U.S. tuna industry began fishing in the region only in the late 1970s and through an industry association, the American Tunaboat Association, negotiated access agreements with some of the islands. But by December 1984 these agreements had all expired. American tunaboats continued to fish in the island EEZs without paying fees and were regarded by the island governments as poachers or pirates. The island governments had little means for enforcing their jurisdiction, but if an American vessel were caught and penalities enforced, U.S. law required stiff trade sanctions against the island governments. The most serious case occurred in 1984 when Solomon Islands seized an American tuna boat, the *Jeanette Diana*, and the United States government reluctantly, but necessarily under its own law, imposed a retaliatory economic embargo.

It was in this context that Kiribati-Soviet negotiations were concluded in August 1985 on an agreement that gave the USSR the right to have 16 vessels fish in its EEZ, but not shore-access rights. In return Kiribati was paid $1.5 million, a relatively sizable inducement for a country whose total budget in 1985 was only $12 million. Kiribati cited the expiration of the American agreement in 1984 as one reason it needed to seek new sources of revenue. The second Soviet agreement was signed with Vanuatu in early 1987 and gave fishing rights to 8 Soviet vessels and allowed shore access, also in return for $1.5 million.

Both agreements expired after a year of operation. The Soviets proposed to renew the Kiribati agreement with a 50 percent reduction in vessels and payments, claiming that their poor fish-take did not justify a continuation on the same scale as earlier. Kiribati refused. Both agreements, however, could still be renewed in the future. PNG signed a three-year fisheries agreement with the Soviet Union in the summer of 1990, with fishing in PNG waters to begin by the end of that year;

and several other island nations have considered establishing fishing arrangements with the Soviet Union.

Despite the rather limited nature of the first agreements, they created considerable concern in foreign policy and defense circles in the Western countries, China, and Japan. Australia took a particularly active role in raising these concerns with the island states. Kiribati and Vanuatu were unmoved, stating that their interests were strictly commercial and pointing out that many other countries, including New Zealand and the United States, had fishing agreements with the Soviet Union. In the Western countries, however, it was feared that such small countries might be especially vulnerable to subversion and political influence. The example of Grenada, a tiny Caribbean nation that had fallen under Cuban influence, had a particularly strong influence on American thinking.

The Soviet fishing initiatives also sparked a fresh concern in the United States about its own troubled fishing relations with the Pacific islands. In 1985, the U.S. government initiated a new approach, and began negotiations with 16 island nations for a regional fisheries agreement, a formula permissible under U.S. law. The island nations coordinated their negotiating position through the Forum Fisheries Agency, and after several rounds of hard bargaining a five-year regional fisheries agreement was reached in October 1986. Under this agreement, the U.S. government would provide $10 million a year in economic assistance, while the U.S. tuna industry would pay $1.75 million annually in license fees and $250,000 a year in technical assistance. Although the island governments were distressed by the further year and a half required for the treaty to be ratified and enabling legislation to be passed by the U.S. Congress, the treaty successfully defused a serious and growing source of friction in U.S.-Pacific island relations.

The island governments saw their multilateral treaty with the United States as bringing greater benefits than the individual licensing arrangements with other foreign fishing fleets. Therefore they have opened negotiations toward a similar agreement with Japan and are interested in agreements with Taiwan and South Korea as well. As of late 1990, however, negotiations with Japan had not progressed, leading to expressions of frustration directed by the island states towards Japan.

With the active assistance of New Zealand, the island states have also launched a campaign to curb drift-net fishing, a technology posing grave dangers to tuna stocks as well as other species. Efforts to date have included the conclusion of a multilateral treaty (the Wellington Convention of November 1989), a UN resolution, and direct pressures on major users of this technology to prohibit or limit its use in the South Pacific. In 1990 the United States banned drift-net fishing in U.S. waters and by U.S. vessels, and acceded to the Wellington Convention, further boosting U.S.-island relations; Japanese resistance to such measures became another issue in Japan-island relations.

Environmental Issues

Environmental issues have been a major area of concern to the Pacific islanders, and a continuing theme in their relations with the outside world. As the inhabitants of ecologically fragile territories, they have a traditional sensitivity to the balance between man and nature. Contact with the Western world and technology has brought with it a series of environmental costs to the islanders, from the degradation resulting from phosphate mining to the wholesale devastation and dislocations of nuclear testing, virtually all of which have been imposed from the outside with little or no real consultation or consideration of the costs. Now the very existence of many of the islands appears to be threatened by the newest environmental dangers.

Anti-nuclear sentiments are of long standing in the island region, partly because the region was used as a testing ground for atmospheric tests by the United States, the United Kingdom, and France; France still conducts underground tests at Mururoa Atoll. Periodic accounts of plans to use the region as a disposal ground for nuclear wastes have also contributed to anti-nuclear sentiment. The islanders fear that leaked radiation from underground testing or storage sites could be carried widely around the region by ocean currents and contaminated fish. The experience of testing was a direct stimulus to island efforts to create a South Pacific nuclear-free zone. In the South Pacific Forum Australia took the lead in drafting a South Pacific Nuclear Free Zone (SPNFZ) Treaty that would meet the islanders' concerns, but still be acceptable in terms of the defense interests of the United States. Completed in 1985, the Treaty of Rarotonga bound signatory Forum members not to develop, produce, test, own, or use nuclear weapons, or allow nuclear weapons testing or storage in their territories, or allow the dumping of nuclear waste materials. Acceptance of port visits by ships capable of carrying nuclear weapons or powered by nuclear generators was left to the discretion of individual Forum members. Since this did not change the status quo, the signatories hoped the treaty would be acceptable to the United States.

Three protocols were attached to the SPNFZ Treaty for signature by the nuclear powers. The first protocol was open for American, British, and French signatures and pledged that these countries would apply the treaty in their own territories. The second and third protocols were open to signature by the five nuclear weapons states. Under the second protocol they pledged not to use or threaten to use nuclear weapons against the signatory island members, and under the third they agreed not to test in the region.

China and the Soviet Union quickly signed and ratified the second and third protocols, although in its initial announcement the Soviet Union qualified its commitment by holding that it would not be bound by the protocols toward any of the signatories that permitted access to nuclear-capable ships or aircraft. Since visits are clearly a matter of national discretion under the treaty, the Soviet qualification was regarded as an attempt to redefine the treaty and was greeted coolly. The USSR subsequently dropped this qualification.

None of the Western nations accepted the protocols. France was not expected to, since this would have meant stopping its underground testing program in Mururoa, something France has refused to contemplate. But the American and British refusals to sign were a source of considerable disappointment to Australia.

In the United States, the treaty was favored by many arms control advocates, who pointed out that the United States had agreed to a similar treaty for Latin America, and by many with special interests in the Pacific region who feared the negative implications for U.S. relations with the region and the positive benefits for the Soviet Union. Congressman Stephen Solarz, chairman of the House Foreign Affairs Subcommittee on Asian and Pacific Affairs, for example, introduced a resolution calling for accession.

The decision of the U.S. administration, however, was against signature, primarily because of concerns that U.S. acceptance might encourage nuclear free zone efforts in such areas as Scandanavia and Southeast Asia, which might be less considerate of U.S. defense interests. U.S. administration spokespersons pointed out that nuclear-free zones were more likely to undermine U.S. defense strategy than Soviet defense strategy because the United States relies more heavily on sea-based deterrents. The United Kingdom refused to sign the protocols for similar reasons. However, the United Kingdom and the United States assured the signatories that their practices in the South Pacific were consistent with the treaty and its protocols.

Environmental concerns, as well as a degree of distrust of the Western nations stemming from the experience with nuclear testing, were also responsible for a wave of criticism and protests from the islands in 1990 of plans by the United States to destroy chemical munitions from the Pacific region and Germany at Johnston Atoll some 800 miles southwest of Hawaii. Island concerns over the move, compounded by lack of advance consultation by the United States, led to a formal statement of opposition issued at the annual Pacific Forum summit meeting, and the dispatch of a joint delegation to Washington. Official American guarantees—ultimately given personally by President Bush at the Honolulu Summit—that the United States planned no further use of Johnston for such purposes, only partially satisfied island opinion.

A final and, for the islands, ultimate environmental concern is the threat of global warming, which through ice-cap melting and sea-level rise could literally erase some of the island countries, such as Tuvalu, from the map. The islands have provided one of the strongest voices calling attention to this phenomenon and arguing for practical action to curb atmosphere-heating emissions even before total scientific certainty can be attained regarding the extent of the danger.

Decolonization

The island countries, particularly through their five United Nations members, have pressed consistently both for the completion of the self-determination process in the Pacific and for international recognition and acceptance of the political forms that have resulted.

The latter effort has been most noteworthy in the case of the four island states that have entered "free association" arrangements with their former administering powers. In recognition of the vulnerability of smaller island states and the near-inevitability of their long-term dependence on external assistance, the island governments have actively lobbied in the international community for acceptance of the free association formula as consistent with sovereign status for these islands. Declarations of support from the South Pacific Forum for the Compacts of Free Association between the Federated States of Micronesia and the Republic of the Marshall Islands and the United States, and acceptance of the two states as full members of the Forum, had a significant impact on attitudes toward these new states in the wider international community.

The decolonization process in the Pacific islands is nearly complete. In addition to the United States, the region's other remaining territorial power of any note is France. In recent years regional decolonization efforts have focused on the French territory of New Caledonia. French policies in the 1960s and 1970s encouraging immigration into New Caledonia as a way of retaining political control of that territory altered the population balance, reducing the indigenous Kanaks to only 43 percent of the present population; but these policies also strengthened indigenous demands for independence. Independence for New Caledonia, or at least the right to choose independence through an act of self-determination, has been supported throughout the island region.

The extent of this support was reflected in the successful effort of the South Pacific Forum members in 1986 to have New Caledonia relisted as a non–self-governing territory under the purview of the United Nations Decolonization Special Committee, obliging France to provide information on the territory and take steps toward decolonization. The French themselves had so listed New Caledonia in 1946, but retracted this step the following year, and no UN action had ever been taken on the territory. In 1979, Kanak leaders began to lobby the South Pacific Forum for support; but following the election in France of François Mitterrand's Socialist Party in March 1981, most of the Forum countries favored giving the new French government time to work out an accommodation.

When Jacques Chirac's conservative government took power in France in March 1986, dependent on support from conservative members of parliament from New Caledonia, the government embarked on a course designed to assure that the territory remained under French control. This had a powerful effect in the Pacific, where it was feared this approach would result in further racial polarization and violence in New Caledonia. When the South Pacific Forum met in August 1986, it unanimously agreed to press for re-inscription of the New Caledonia issue at the United Nations, a step pushed particularly strongly by the Melanesian states. Lobbying by the Forum members, including Australia and New Zealand, resulted in a UN General Assembly vote of 89 to 24 in favor of the action. The Forum kept up the pressure at its next meeting in May 1987, urging the Decolonization Special Committee to recommend that the General Assembly adopt a resolution supporting a UN-sponsored referendum consistent with "universally accepted principles and practices of self-determination and independence." In December 1987, the General Assembly adopted by a vote of 69 to 29 a resolution reaffirming New Caledonia's right to independence and self-determination.

In the French presidential elections of May 1988, Chirac lost his bid to replace Mitterrand, and in the parliament a new Socialist Party government, led by Prime Minister Michel Rocard, replaced Chirac's conservative government. This French domestic change, coupled with rising violence in New Caledonia where ugly incidents resulted in the deaths of 21 Melanesians and 3 French gendarmes just before the elections, led to another French change of approach toward the Pacific island territory. The Matignon Accords, approved by the late separatist leader Jean-Marie Tjibaou and by the political leader of the New Caledonian French settler community, Jacques Lafleur, created a federation of three self-ruling provinces, two of which would have Kanak political majorities. No vote on independence would take place until 1998.

With the principal Kanak leaders supporting the Matignon plan, the

Forum countries expressed their approval. Nevertheless, the potential for a new outbreak of political strife in racially polarized New Caledonia remains, and despite approval of the plan in a French referendum in November 1988 purposely designed by the Rocard government to make further policy reversals more difficult, the vagaries of French politics could produce new and less happy approaches in Paris.

Although the decolonization issue in the other French territories in the Pacific, French Polynesia and Wallis and Futuna, has been quiescent by contrast with New Caledonia, there are signs that point to possible greater attention in the future. An active political movement by indigenous Polynesians in French Polynesia, combined with resentment of the dominant position of French officials and settlers, led to riots in the capital of Papeete in 1987 and continued activism since. In October 1990, Solomon Islands called for the re-inscription of French Polynesia on the UN list of non–self-governing territories, possibly signaling the start of a process parallel to that in New Caldeonia. The combination of the nuclear testing and self-determination issues in French Polynesia could give this situation resonance throughout the islands.

CONCLUSIONS

The coming of independence and the growth of multipolarity on the global stage have brought new, more diverse, and more intense patterns of international relations to the Pacific island region. Particularly after the mid-1980s there was a series of initiatives arising from the islands or directed toward the islands from the outside. These included the Pacific initiatives on the nuclear-free zone and New Caledonia and the growth of activity in the region by the United States, the Soviet Union, Japan, China, Australia, New Zealand, and France. Other nations, including Indonesia, Malaysia, Canada, Taiwan, and South Korea, have to lesser extents increased their diplomatic and assistance activities in the region.

Because the island entities are so small, this new international attention can be almost overwhelming. Ironically, although the Western powers and Japan hope to promote political stability in the region by increased aid programs and contacts, such efforts can be counterproductive without a sound understanding of the region's special characteristics and development needs. For the island economies, the concepts and modalities of outside assistance might be completely different than those for large developing nations, the model for most American or Japanese aid programs. Moreover, competing outside interests may serve to intensify internal political and social tensions. Well-meaning programs intended to promote regional stability may have the opposite effect by forcing an unsustainable pace of change. It is particularly important, therefore, that as the island region broadens its external contacts and intensifies contacts with countries such as Japan and the United States that do not have long histories of close relations with most of the island region, there be an effective process of dialogue and learning. Such a process is most needed to foster peaceful relations between the island countries and the Pacific Rim.

REFERENCES AND SUGGESTED READING

Australia's Relations with the South Pacific. The Parliament of the Commonwealth of Australia, Joint Committee on Foreign Affairs, Defence and Trade, 1989.

Baker, Richard. "International Relations of the Southwest Pacific—New Visions and Voices," in the *Asia-Pacific Report 1990-91: A New Pattern of International Relations*. Charles E. Morrison, editor, Honolulu: East-West Center, forthcoming.

Biddick, Thomas V. "Diplomatic Rivalry in the South Pacific: The PRC and Taiwan," in *Asian Survey*, Vol. XXIX, No. 8, August 1989, pp. 800-815.

Dorrance, John C. *Oceania and the United States: An Analysis of U.S. Interests and Policy in the South Pacific*. The National Defense University Press, Washington, D.C., 1980.

Hegarty, David. "International Relations and Security in the South Pacific," paper presented at the Conference on ASEAN and the Pacific Islands, East-West Center, Honolulu, September 1987.

"Problems in Paradise: United States Interests in the South Pacific." Report of a Congressional Delegation to the South Pacific, August 15-16, 1989. Committee on Foreign Affairs, Washington, D.C., May 1990.

Thambipillai, Pushpa and Daniel C. Matuszewski, editors. *The Soviet Union and the Asia-Pacific Region: Views from the Region*. New York: Praeger, 1989.

Towards a Pacific Island Community. Report of the South Pacific Policy Review Group, Wellington, New Zealand, May 1990.

6
The Pacific Islands in the Pacific Community

With the regaining of sovereignty, a comparatively recent phenomenon, most Pacific island countries continue to rely primarily on the former colonial powers for financial and technical assistance and on regional cooperation as a vehicle for achieving some of their development objectives and for dealing with the outside world. Partly reflecting this orientation, they have not yet taken an active part in the major cooperative initiatives that are taking place in the broader Asia-Pacific region. However, the Pacific islands have much to gain from a closer involvement in Pacific Basin economic cooperation as well as closer contact with other regional groupings such as ASEAN.

This chapter deals briefly with such broader Pacific cooperation, represented by the Association of South East Asian Nations (ASEAN) and the wider Asia Pacific Economic Cooperation (APEC) initiative, and the question of how the Pacific islands can play a more effective role in these processes.

THE BROAD PICTURE

The Pacific island entities occupy the center—a vast one—of the Pacific Basin (or Asia-Pacific region), a region fringed by some of the most powerful and dynamic economies in the world. The United States and Japan are the leading actors, each of whose scale of industrial production and GNP surpass those of any other single economy, while the NIEs—Singapore, Hong Kong, Taiwan, and South Korea—are among the fastest growing economies in the world. Several other developing countries, notably Thailand and Malaysia, appear set to join the NIEs.

The reasons for the economic success of Asian economies such as Japan and the NIEs are varied and by no means clear. But several causal factors appear to have played a significant part in this success, including increased productivity in agriculture, effective land reforms, high national savings rates, reliance on free-market forces as a mechanism for the allocation of resources, and strong export orientation.

To all intents and purposes, however, the remarkable growth experience of many Pacific Rim countries has affected the Pacific islands only marginally. In fact, it can be argued that the successes of the rim, especially the NIEs, have had a perverse effect on the Pacific islands in certain areas. For example, rapid economic transformation of some Asian economies has tended to undermine the competitive position of the islands and made them less attractive for foreign investment.

Significant economic contact between the Pacific islands and Pacific Rim countries has taken place in only a few areas and among a limited number of countries. Aside from the United States, Japan has been a leading actor—especially in fishing and trade. In trade, Japan has been a leading importer of mineral products, primarily nickel and copper, and forestry products; and Japan exports to the islands a wide range of consumer and capital goods. As previously noted, Japan has also become very active as an aid donor and investor.

Extensive fishing is also carried out by other Pacific Rim countries, including the United States, Taiwan, South Korea, and Indonesia, but only Singapore and the United States are important trade partners. Trade flows are heavily weighted toward consumer goods. Technical training of Pacific islanders has taken place in several Asian countries. Malaysia has shown increasing interest in investing in the Pacific. Since the coups in Fiji, Malaysia and several other members of ASEAN have sought to establish closer contacts with that country and have provided limited economic assistance.

The failure to develop more effective contacts between the Pacific islands region and the Pacific Rim countries can be explained partly by the limited size and economic significance of the Pacific islands. The developing countries of the Pacific Rim have sought dynamic growth through establishing wide contacts with the larger economic entities outside the Pacific Basin. The islands, on the other hand, have tended to limit their economic dealings to those metropolitan powers with whom they have historical ties, especially as sources of foreign aid, training, and trade. This lack of broader contact has meant that the small Pacific islands have not been able to be active participants in the dynamic processes taking place around the Pacific Rim. The marginal economic role of the island entities is also reflected in their limited participation in organized economic cooperation efforts in the Pacific Basin.

RELATIONS WITH ASEAN

The closest organizational counterpart of the Pacific islands group in the larger region, and the most logical candidate for broader cooperation with the islands is ASEAN, established in 1967 and consisting of

Indonesia, Malaysia, the Philippines, Singapore, Thailand, and Brunei (as of 1984). As immediate neighbors the two groups also have a direct common interest in such areas as control of fisheries and other deep sea resources, environmental regulation, etc. The island states have made a number of approaches to ASEAN and its members, and the interest of the ASEAN states in the Pacific has increased markedly in recent years. Both regional groupings now are clearly eager to know more about the other and to identify areas of common interest as a basis for closer interaction and cooperation.

Present trade activity between the ASEAN members and the Pacific islands is small. In 1986, total trade flows approximated only $350 million, with exports from ASEAN to the Pacific islands totaling $240 million and imports by ASEAN, $110 million (Thambipillai, 1987: 15). Over 90 percent of exports from ASEAN to the Pacific is accounted for by Singapore—and the major markets are Papua New Guinea and Fiji. ASEAN's imports from the Pacific islands are more evenly distributed but principally come from Solomon Islands, Papua New Guinea, and Nauru. Of the ASEAN countries, only Malaysia has been active in investment in the islands.

Other links, mainly bilateral, have developed over time. ASEAN's relations have been particularly close with Papua New Guinea, which, as previously indicated, shares a common border with the Indonesian province of Irian Jaya. PNG attends ASEAN gatherings as an observer, and the question of full membership has been raised from time-to-time. Diplomatic representation has been established between several ASEAN members and Papua New Guinea and Fiji, while Singapore, Malaysia, and Brunei share membership in the British Commonwealth with several Pacific island states.

A number of initiatives have been launched to improve relations between the two groupings. Consultations between ASEAN and the South Pacific Forum began in 1980 when the secretary-general of ASEAN visited the Forum Secretariat in Suva for discussions on furthering relations between the two. In the same year the director of SPEC visited the ASEAN national secretariats in Bangkok and Kuala Lumpur. A formal visit by the Forum Secretariat director to the ASEAN Secretariat in Jakarta followed in 1981, in line with a South Pacific Forum directive to pursue dialogue on "meaningful and practical areas of cooperation between ASEAN and the South Pacific Forum" (Pryor, 1987:20). Opportunities were identified for cooperation in several areas: trade, shipping, fish products, energy, and investment.

At the annual Forum meetings in the mid- and late-1980s the interest of Forum leaders in closer cooperation with ASEAN was reiterated. Most recently, the 1989 Forum meeting mandated the Forum secretary-general to renew contacts with the ASEAN countries with a view to identifying areas and channels of cooperation.

Several specific activities involving the Forum Secretariat are worth noting. In cooperation with the Asian and Pacific Development Center (APDC), the Forum Secretariat in 1986 initiated the so-called ASEAN-South Pacific Investment Study to examine the investment environment in the countries of the two regions, regional complementarities in the investment area, and possibilities for joint ventures. An investment directory has been compiled, which provides basic information on investment opportunities and facilities in the two regions; and a total of seven volumes has been published incorporating the findings from the study.

The Forum Secretariat in 1986 hosted a meeting entitled "Forum on ASEAN-South Pacific Investment Promotion," attended by representatives of governments and the private sector from ASEAN and Forum island members. Participants concluded that the best prospects for future interregional investment cooperation were in marine resources, agriculture-based industries, forestry, manufacturing-marketing, tourism, and mining (SPEC, 1988:14). In promoting cooperation in these fields it was agreed that the private sector should take a leading part.

Other organizations have also helped explore possibilities for an enhanced relationship between the Pacific islands and ASEAN. For example, ESCAP has undertaken research into possibilities for increased economic and technical cooperation between the two regional groupings and their constituent countries. In 1987 and 1989, the East-West Center and Indonesia's Center for Strategic and International Studies sponsored workshops for representatives from ASEAN and the Pacific islands that focused on current developments in the two regions and areas of potential interregional cooperation.

Apart from the economic and related advantages that could be realized through closer contacts between the two regions, both sides recognize that each can benefit from the other from their respective experience in promoting regional cooperation and economic integration. For example, the Pacific islands can learn much from ASEAN's experience in encouraging economic and trade cooperation through preferential trading and industrial cooperation schemes. These ASEAN initiatives have had only limited success, but their record—and the obstacles faced in the course of implementation—could be valuable for the Pacific islands as they contemplate their own future development efforts.

In 1989 the Forum took a leaf from ASEAN's book by inviting representatives of the major donor states to "dialogue" meetings with island leaders following the annual Forum meetings. This practice, which is based on ASEAN's annual post-ministerial conferences with the foreign ministers of the leading industrial powers, will most likely also become an annual event. ASEAN can learn as well from the Pacific islands' experience in regional cooperation—from such examples as the negotiation of regional fisheries arrangements, environmental protection conventions, and non-nuclear agreements.

THE ISLANDS AND PACIFIC ECONOMIC COOPERATION

For the long term, even more important to the Pacific islands than cooperation with the neighboring ASEAN grouping is to find an appropriate means of involvement in the broader efforts at Asia-Pacific regional cooperation. Efforts to create an organizational framework for region-wide cooperation first led to the establishment of the nongovernmental Pacific Economic Cooperation Conference (PECC) in 1980, and most recently have led to the intergovernmental Asia Pacific Economic Cooperation (APEC) initiative launched by Australia through a meeting of 12 regional countries in Canberra in November 1989.

The PECC process brings together three participating groups— business and industry, government, and academics—in task forces and larger conferences to discuss regional issues of common interest. Among the subject areas are trade, natural resource development (especially agriculture, fisheries, minerals, and energy), transportation, investment, education, and training. Essentially consultative, PECC seeks to achieve consensus on substantive issues discussed and to tread cautiously in its proceedings, taking account of the sensitivities and special interests of its individual members and subgroups.

From the outset, the organizers of PECC recognized the fact that Pacific islands, along with other developing countries including the ASEAN group, face special problems, needs, and limited resource bases that must be taken into account. At its inaugural meeting in Canberra in 1980, PECC participants emphasized the need to accommodate the "particular interests" of the Pacific islands and, in doing so, to proceed cautiously to ensure that their "integrity" was not impaired.

However, Pacific island participation in the PECC process has been minimal; rarely have there been more than two or three Pacific island representatives at PECC conferences. At the same time, PECC has given little attention to the Pacific, perhaps largely because of the region's limited economic significance combined with a relatively quiescent political tradition.

To date, only two PECC activities have directly benefited the Pacific islands. The first was in fisheries. Stimulated by the Philippines, a consultative body—the Pacific Fisheries Consultative Committee—has been established under the PECC framework involving the ASEAN countries and the Forum island members. The purpose of the committee is to provide a center for consultation and exchange of information between the fisheries representatives of the two regional groupings as a means of promoting the development of their respective fisheries sectors.

The 1988 session of the PECC established a task force, primarily supported by the United States, Japanese, Taiwan, and South Korean national committees, to study means of promoting expanded trade and investment between the PECC members and the islands. Despite a number of meetings and discussions with island representatives, however, as of late 1990 the work of the task force had shown little concrete result and the effort was in suspension.

One evident problem in PECC-island cooperation has been the difficulty of organizing an authoritative island partner. The Forum Secretariat appears to be the appropriate body to promote Pacific island participation in PECC activities, but the Forum Secretariat can only make commitments with the approval of the island leaders at the annual South Pacific Forum gatherings. Operational cooperation between a committee-based non-governmental organization and a group of international civil servants is inherently awkward, but the alternative of such a committee working with over a dozen individual governments is equally inefficient.

A similar but still more complicated problem affects island representation in the APEC process. APEC was explicitly launched to provide a regional intergovernmental forum in which the leading economic actors of the region could consult on major economic trends and issues affecting them all. Twelve governments were represented at the inaugural APEC meeting in Canberra: the six ASEAN member states, the United States, Canada, Japan, South Korea, Australia, and New Zealand (possible participation by China, Hong Kong, and Taiwan is one of the major organizational issues now before the group). An additional meeting was held in Singapore in 1990, and follow-on meetings are now scheduled for 1991 in Korea and 1992 in the United States.

The Pacific island states were represented at the inaugural meeting by the Forum secretary-general, who was invited as an observer. The secretary-general, however, is not able to speak authoritatively for the island leaders. But, on the other hand, the inclusion of all the island states in the APEC process would be unwieldy and result in domination at least of the numbers if not the agendas by the region's smallest economies. Some of the larger island states, particularly Papua New Guinea, would like to participate in the APEC process in their own right, which would not solve and could in some respects even further complicate the problem of representation for the smaller island states.

Some kind of rotational representation arrangement may be worked out, but at best such an arrangement would still be awkward for the islands. Under any representation formula, the islands will remain handicapped by their extreme shortages of expert manpower and the resources necessary to support meaningful participation.

So we are left with a dilemma. The island states urgently need to expand their interaction with the wider regional economy, and thereby to increase understanding in the region of their special circumstances and needs. Inclusion in regional processes such as APEC would be a valuable step in this direction. But given their limited human and other resources, the island countries see little real benefit from participation in large discussion forums or more generalized economic participation arrangements. From the islands' perspective, the best way for the APEC process to accommodate their special economic needs is through the creation of specific mechanisms—on the model of the SPARTECA trade preferences with Australia and New Zealand or the Lome Convention assistance program of the European Community—that will provide direct, practical economic benefits. The challenge—to both the islands and to the rim countries—is to carve such a middle path that offers tangible benefits without unsustainable burdens.

CONCLUDING COMMENTS

By comparison with many other developing regions, the Pacific islands have made considerable progress in facing up to the challenges of development and in maintaining their political integrity despite a relatively short experience as independent or self-governing entities. Their efforts to promote economic growth, supported fairly heavily by the international aid community, have been extensive and, at least for the larger island countries, should result in substantially enhanced abilities to generate self-sustaining growth and self-reliance. Regional cooperation is relatively advanced and provides a basis for the Pacific islands to join forces in promoting their collective interest vis-a-vis the wider world and in achieving certain national objectives in key areas of development. Their relations with the larger outside powers have been in flux in recent years, but have been expanding and offer further opportunities for advancing island economic and political interests.

With increasing interdependence among the countries of the Pacific Basin, despite their remoteness and small size, the Pacific islands will ineluctably be drawn even more closely into the wider world. This prospect can be both a curse and a blessing. Greater interaction with the outside world can mean a more intense exposure to externally induced instabilities and can open the way to even greater aid dependence. On the other hand, the benefits of closer linkages with the outside world are manifold: they include improved access to development finance and other vital inputs, enlarged markets for the region's products, expansion of education, and training opportunities.

REFERENCES AND SUGGESTED READING

The Canadian Chamber of Commerce. *Report of the Fifth Pacific Economic Cooperation Conference*. Vancouver, Canada, 1986.

Curran, Teresa M. "Establishing an Island Focus: An Analysis of the Committee of Pacific Economic Cooperation and Pacific Island Nations." Unpublished report prepared for the U.S. National Committee for Pacific Economic Cooperation, Harvard University, Massachusetts, 1988.

Drysdale, P. "South Pacific Trade and Development Assistance." Unpublished paper presented at the meeting on "Pacific Cooperation and Development." Apia, Western Samoa, 1987.

Pryor, Pamela, T.I. "The Pacific Islands and ASEAN: Prospects for 1987 Interregional Cooperation." Paper presented at the workshop on "ASEAN and the Pacific Islands." East-West Center, Resource Systems Institute, Honolulu, 1987.

South Pacific Bureau of Economic Cooperation. *Forum on ASEAN-South Pacific Investment Promotion: Summary Record*. Suva, Fiji, 1988.

Thambipillai, P. "ASEAN and the Pacific Islands: Bilateral and 1987 Multilateral Relations." Paper presented at the workshop on "ASEAN and the Pacific Islands." East-West Center, Resource Systems Institute, Honolulu, 1987.

APPENDIXES

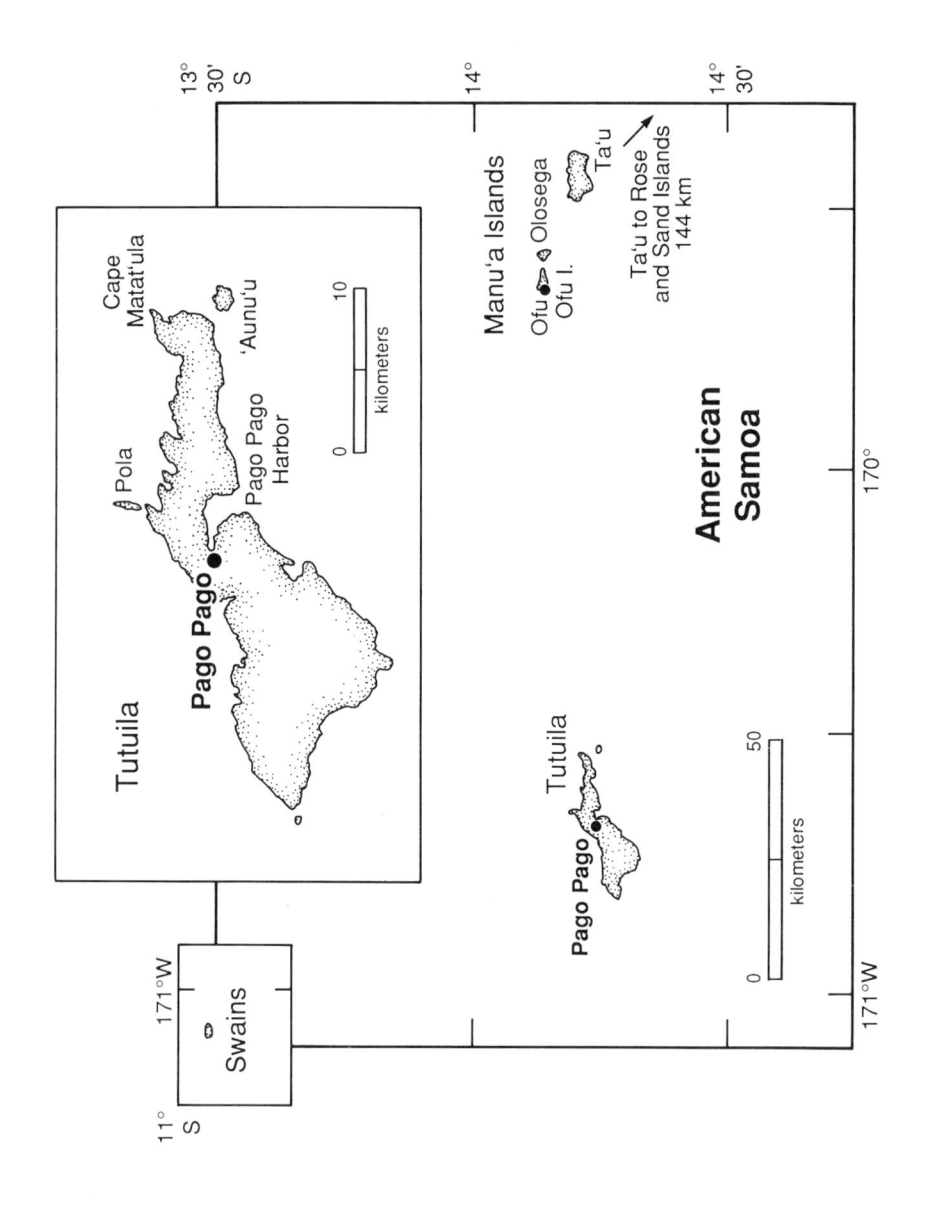

APPENDIX 1
Pacific Island Profiles and Maps

AMERICAN SAMOA

Geography

American Samoa is made up of five main islands and two atolls located east of the 171st meridian of W longitude. The total land area is 197 km^2 and sea area encompasses 390,000 km^2. The main island is Tutuila, where the administrative center Pago Pago is located. The islands were formed from the remains of extinct volcanoes leaving central mountain ranges with limited coastal plains. American Samoa's neighbors are Western Samoa to the west, Tokelau to the north, Cook Islands to the east, and Niue and Tonga to the south.

Population

The population is around 36,700, with a density of 186 per km^2. American Samoans are Polynesians, ethnically the same as Western Samoans, and speak the same language. They have free entry into the United States; an estimated 65,000 have migrated to the U.S. West Coast while some 20,000 American Samoans reside in Hawaii.

Politics

American Samoa is an unorganized, unincorporated territory of the United States under the general supervision of the Department of Interior. It is considered "unorganized" because it does not have a constitution approved by the U.S. Congress. There are three branches of government: the executive headed by a popularly elected governor who exercises authority under the U.S. Secretary of the Interior; a bicameral legislature of 18 senators chosen in accordance with Samoan *matai* custom and 20 representatives elected by popular vote; and a judiciary.

Economy

The U.S. government is the biggest employer, followed by the tuna canning industry. Tourism is the next largest cash earner. There is a thriving fishing industry, but the economy is heavily dependent on assistance from the U.S. government. GNP is $55.8 million, and per capita GNP $1,845 (1982 figures).

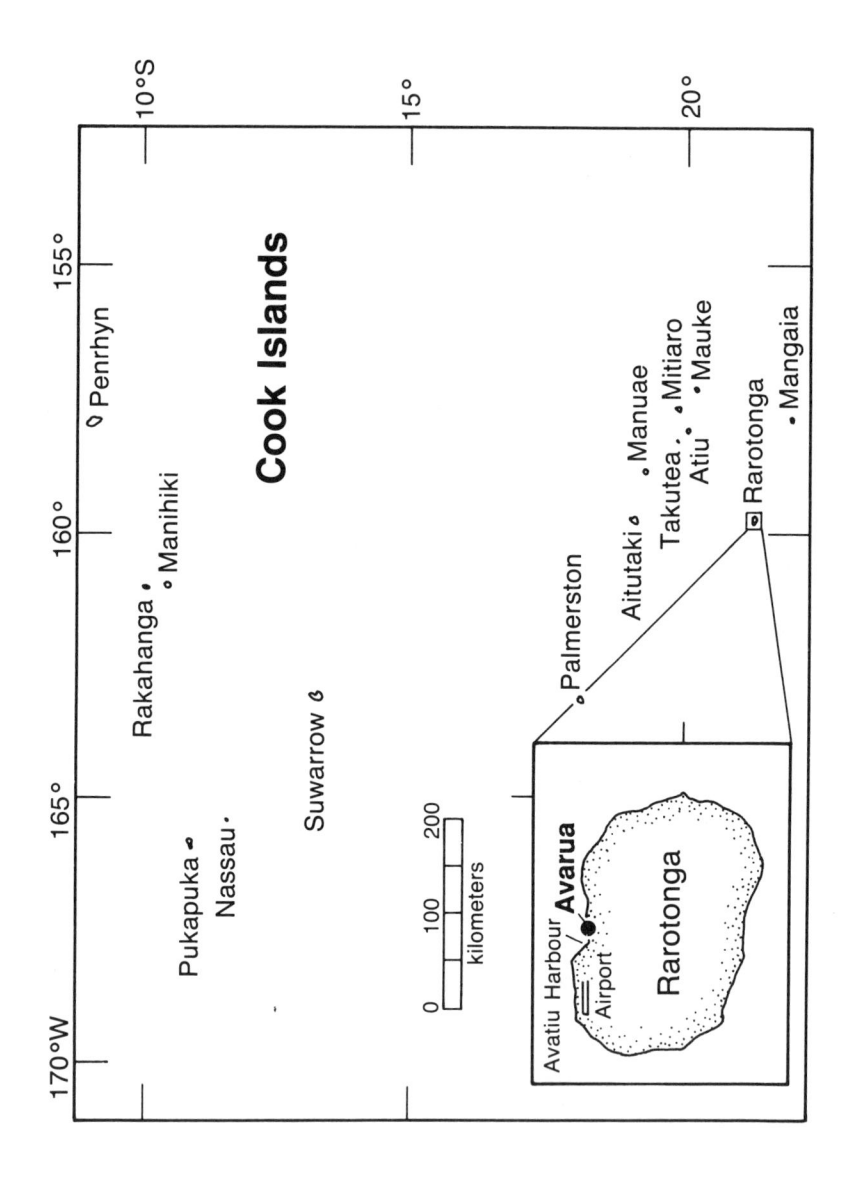

COOK ISLANDS

Geography

Cook Islands is located between 156 and 167 degrees W longitude and between 8 and 23 degrees S latitude. The nearest neighbors are French Polynesia to the east, Niue and American Samoa to the west. Cook Islands comprise 15 islands with a total land area of 240 km² in a sea area of 2.2 million km². The main island is Rarotonga on which the capital Avarua is located. The islands are a combination of volcanic islands and low-lying coral atolls.

Population

The population of Cook Islands is about 18,000, with a population density of 75 per km². Most of the people live on the main island of Rarotonga. The people are mostly Polynesian. Cook Islands Maori and English are the main languages. Because of limited economic opportunity in the islands, many Cook Islanders migrate to New Zealand.

Politics

Cook Islands was administered by New Zealand until 1965. At that time it became self-governing in free association with New Zealand, which is responsible for defense and foreign affairs. Cook Islands is a parliamentary democracy headed by a prime minister.

Economy

The economy of Cook Islands is mainly subsistence agriculture and fishing, with tourism also playing an important role. The primary exports are copra, fruit juices, fruits, and vegetables. The GNP of Cook Islands is $20 million (1985) and the GNP per capita is $1,360.

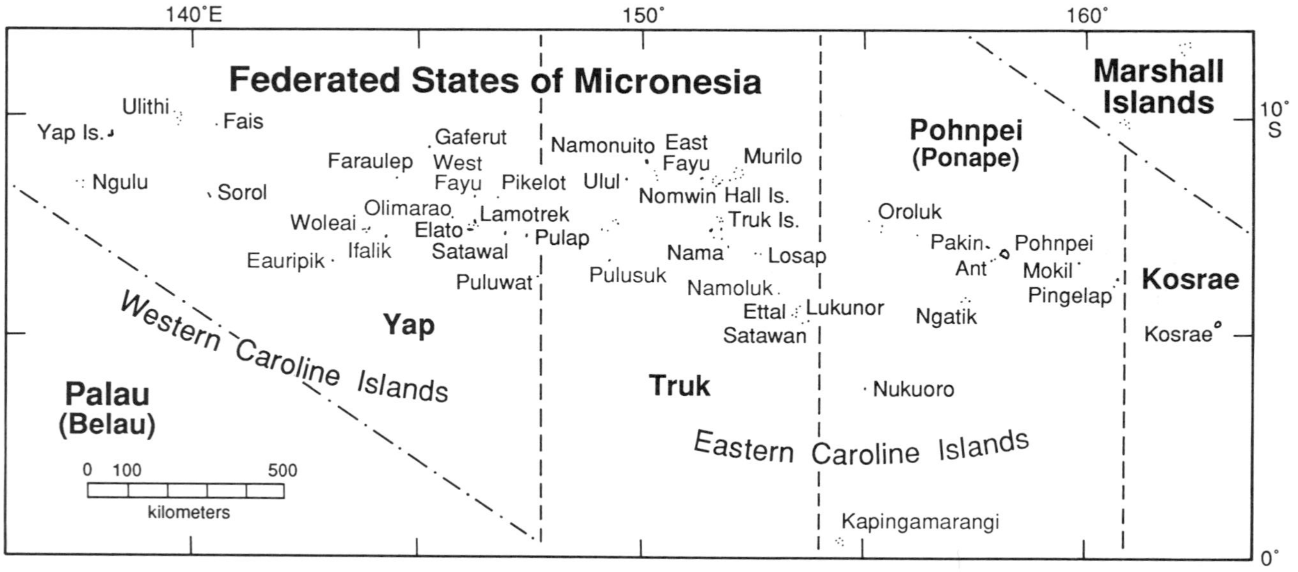

140°E
150°
160°
10° S
0°
Federated States of Micronesia
Marshall Islands
Pohnpei (Ponape)
Kosrae
Yap
Truk
Palau (Belau)
Western Caroline Islands
Eastern Caroline Islands
Yap Is.
Ulithi
Fais
Ngulu
Sorol
Faraulep
Gaferut
West Fayu
Woleai
Olimarao
Elato
Lamotrek
Ifalik
Eauripik
Satawal
Pikelot
Puluwat
Pulap
Namonuito
Ulul
East Fayu
Murilo
Nomwin
Hall Is.
Truk Is.
Pulusuk
Nama
Losap
Namoluk
Ettal
Lukunor
Satawan
Oroluk
Pakin
Ant
Pohnpei
Mokil
Pingelap
Ngatik
Nukuoro
Kapingamarangi
Kosrae
0 100 500
kilometers

FEDERATED STATES OF MICRONESIA (FSM)

Geography

The Federated States of Micronesia (FSM) is located between 0 and 14 degrees N latitude and 136 and 166 degrees E longitude. Its neighbors are Guam to the north, Palau to the west, and the Marshall Islands to the east. FSM is made up of hundreds of islands that range from lush high volcanic islands to low-lying coral atolls. These islands comprise a land area of 700.8 km^2 scattered over hundreds of thousands of square kilometers of ocean.

Population

The population of FSM is about 93,000. The people are mostly Micronesian with some Polynesians and Americans. The population density is about 133 per km^2. Languages are mainly Micronesian dialects and English.

Politics

FSM is divided into the four states of Pohnpei, Chuuk (Truk), Yap, and Kosrae. The national government, based on the American system, is located on Pohnpei in the capital of Kolonia. FSM's colonial history includes rule by Spain, Germany, Japan, and finally the United States when it became a United Nations Trust Territory at the end of World War II. FSM became self-governing in free association with the United States in 1986.

Economy

The GNP of FSM is $106 million (1983). The economy of FSM is based mainly on traditional agriculture and fishing. There are very few exports from FSM; the main products are copra, black pepper, and fish.

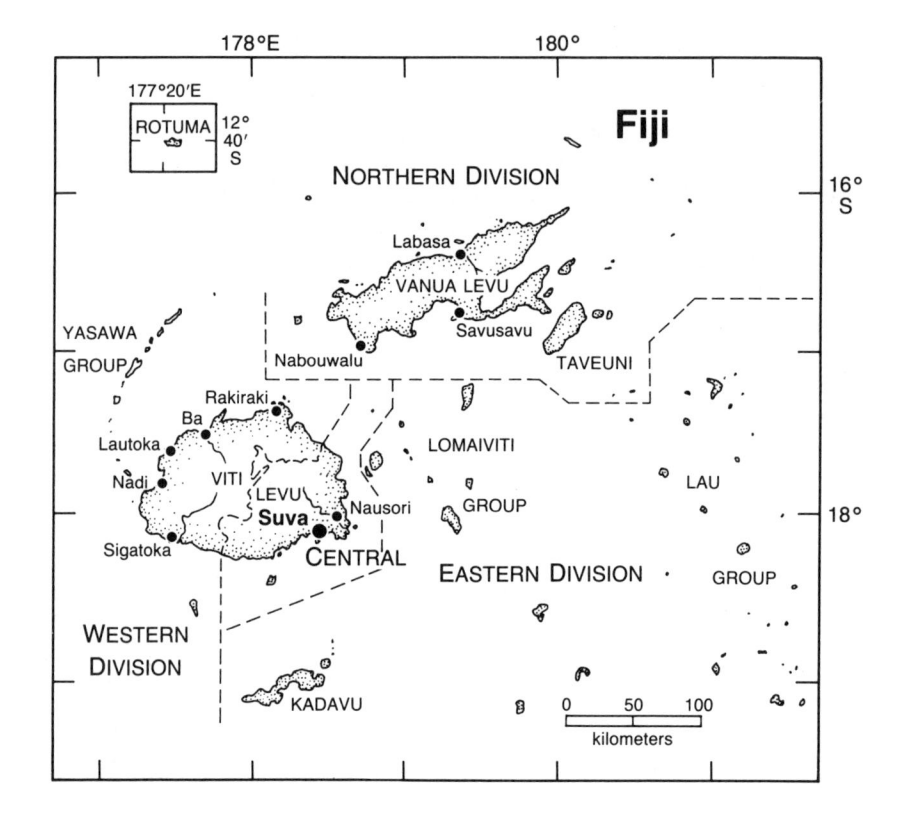

FIJI

Geography

The Republic of Fiji is located between 15 and 22 degrees S latitude and 177 degrees W and 175 degrees E longitude. Its neighbors are Vanuatu to the west, Tonga to the southeast, and Western Samoa to the northeast. Fiji is made up of hundreds of islands comprising 18,272 km² with a sea area of about 193,000 km². The main islands are Vanua Levu and Viti Levu, where the capital Suva is located. There are large volcanic islands and many smaller coral atolls.

Population

The population of Fiji is about 732,000 with a density of 40 per km². Most of the people live on the island of Viti Levu. The population is comprised of 46 percent ethnic Fijians (Melanesians), 48 percent ethnic Indians, and 8 percent others. Languages widely spoken are Fijian, Hindustani, and English.

Politics

Fiji was administered by the United Kingdom until independence in 1970. At that time a parliamentary democracy was established with a prime minister as the head of government. Parliament was suspended following two military coups in 1987, and Fiji became a republic in October of that year. A new constitution was promulgated in 1990 and elections under the new constitution were scheduled for 1991.

Economy

The GNP of Fiji is about $1,190 million (1989) with a GNP per capita of $1,572. Agriculture, tourism, and manufacturing are the major components of the economy. Much of the population is in the subsistence farming sector. Major exports are sugar, textiles, gold, copra, fish, and timber.

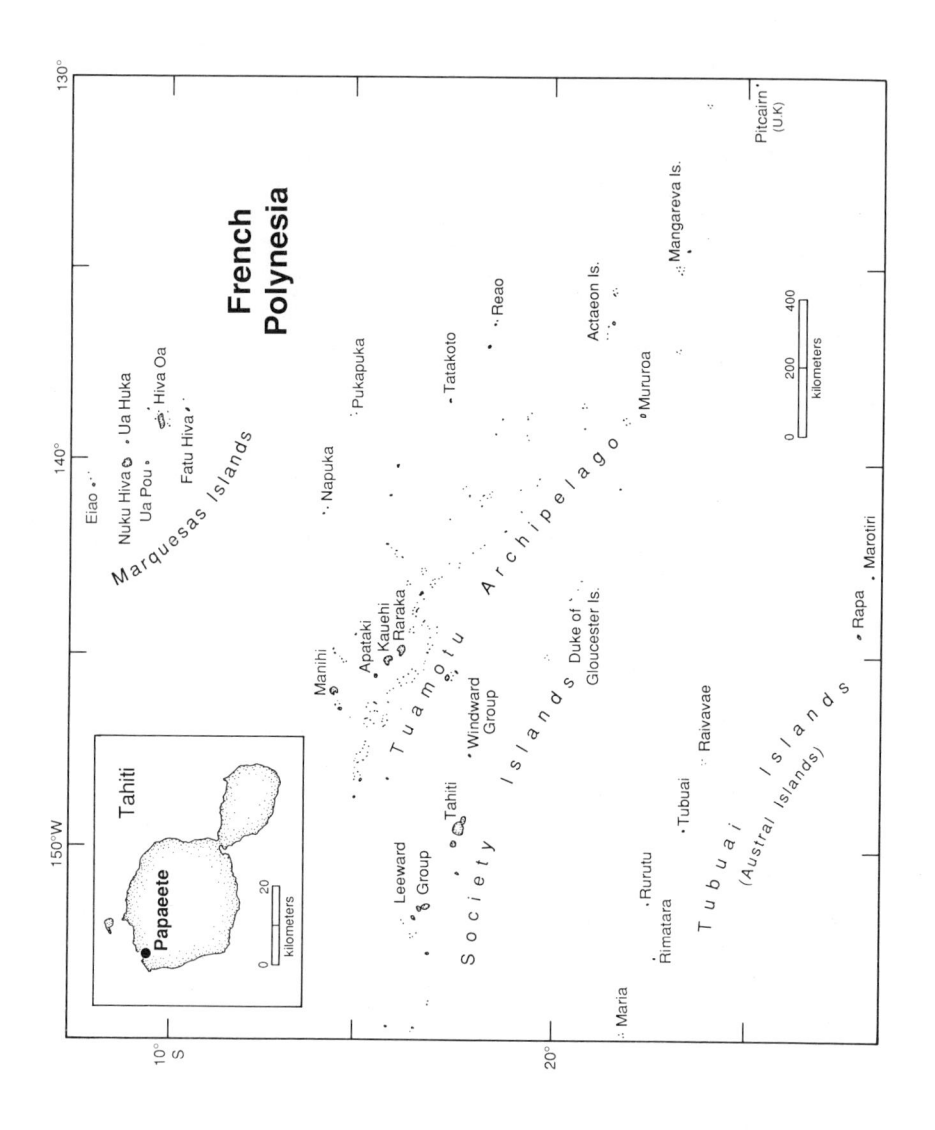

FRENCH POLYNESIA

Geography

French Polynesia contains five main island groups (Society Islands, Tuamotu Archipelago, Gambier Islands, Austral Islands, and Marquesas Islands) totaling some 130 islands extending from 7 to 29 degrees S latitude and from 131 to 156 degrees W longitude. The largest island is Tahiti where the capital Papeete is located. Total land area is 4,000 km² in an area of 4 million km² of ocean. Most of the islands are archipelagoes composed of now extinct volcanoes with high mountainous formations and deep valleys. French Polynesia's closest neighbors are Cook Islands to the west and Kiribati to the northwest.

Population

The population of French Polynesia is 176,800, with two-thirds living on Tahiti. Population density is 44 per km². Polynesians constitute about 70 percent of the population with Europeans (15 percent), part-Europeans (8 percent) and Chinese (7 percent) making up the remainder. All Polynesians and most of the Chinese are French citizens. The official languages are French and Tahitian.

Politics

French Polynesia is an overseas territory of the French Republic and is represented in Paris by a senator, elected by the local political bodies, and two deputies, who are elected by direct popular vote. The French Republic is represented in French Polynesia by a high commissioner. Local political bodies consist of a Territorial Assembly of 30 members (elected by popular vote) who in turn elect 7 members of the Government Council.

Economy

Except for tourism, which plays an important role in employment in the territory, the economy of French Polynesia is dominated by French government spending, half of which goes to the military and much of the rest to French civil servants. The nuclear testing facilities that were opened in 1963 on Mururoa atoll increased trade and building activities, and brought an influx of French settlers. The main agricultural products are copra, coconut oil, vanilla, and coffee. There is potential in fisheries and seabed mineral deposits, but these remain undeveloped. GNP is $1,370 million and per capital GNP $7,480 (1985 figures).

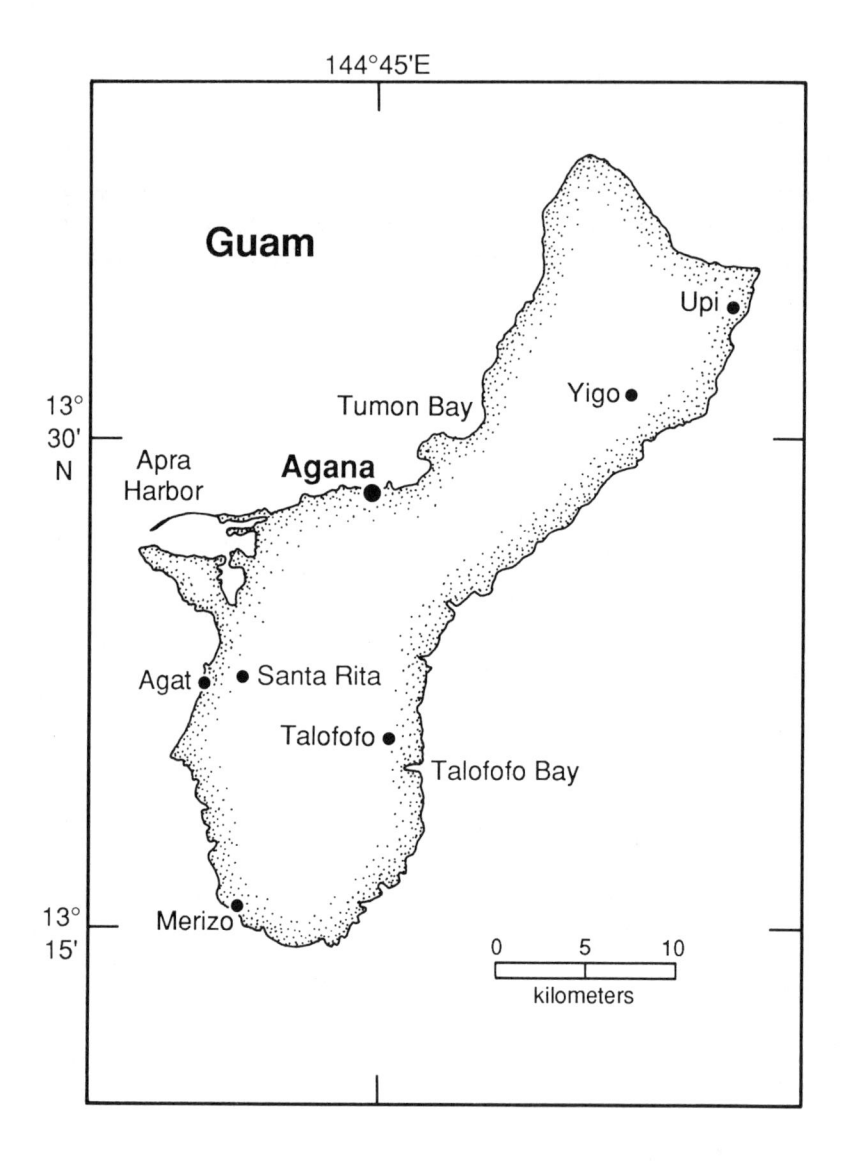

Guam

- Upi
- Yigo
- Tumon Bay
- Apra Harbor
- **Agana**
- Agat
- Santa Rita
- Talofofo
- Talofofo Bay
- Merizo

144°45'E
13°30'N
13°15'

0 5 10 kilometers

GUAM

Geography

Guam is a 549 km² volcanic island located at the southern-most end of the Mariana archipelago at 13 degrees 26 minutes N latitude and 144 degrees 43 minutes E longitude. Guam also has a 218,000 km² sea area and has the Northern Marianas to the north and the Federated States of Micronesia to the south as its closest neighbors.

Population

The population of Guam is 119,800 and the density 248 per km². Ninety percent of the population lives in the capital city of Agana. Forty-two percent can trace their ancestry to native Chamorros (a mixed race with Micronesian, Filipino, and Spanish blood), 21 percent to the Philippines, while 24 percent are military personnel and dependents of the U.S. Department of Defense. English and Chamorro are the official languages.

Politics

Guam is an unincorporated territory of the United States under the general supervision of the Department of Interior. There are three branches of government—the executive headed by a governor elected by popular vote; a unicameral legislature of 21 senators elected by four legislative districts; and the judiciary. A non-voting delegate to the U.S. House of Representatives elected by popular vote represents the islanders in Washington, D.C. A 1988 poll showed the majority of Guamanians favor a Commonwealth arrangement with the right of self-determination for Chamorros and limited powers of the United States to alter the Commonwealth status.

Economy

Guam is heavily dependent on imports and relies on the U.S. government for financial support. Tourism is the most important industry in the private sector and the second major revenue earner after federal government expenditures (including the military). There is potential for fisheries development since Guam is located near productive fishing grounds. GNP is $670 million and per capita GNP is $5,470 (1985 figures).

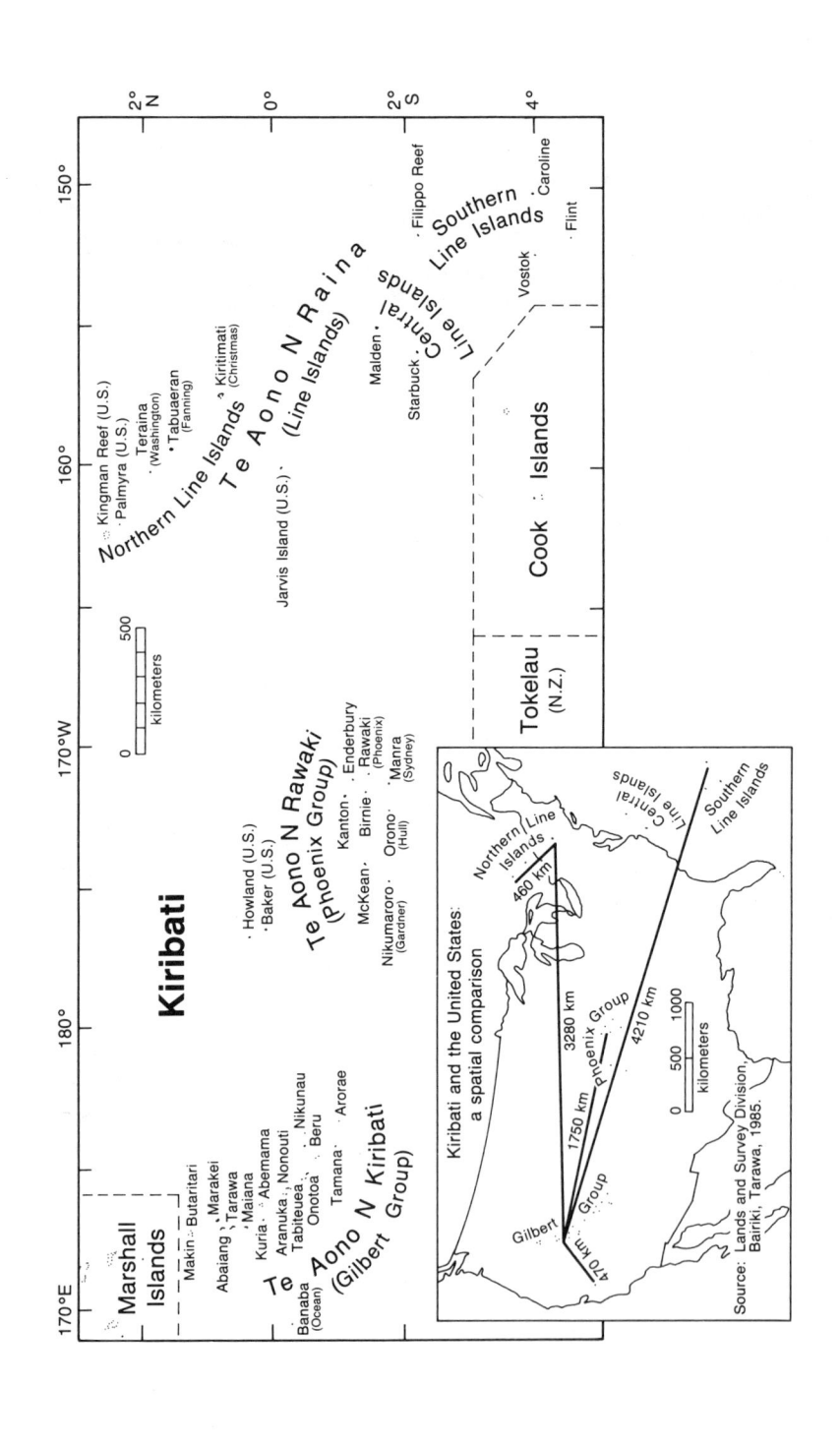

Kiribati

Marshall Islands

Makin · · Butaritari
Abaiang · · Marakei
  · Tarawa
   · Maiana
Kuria · · Abemama
Aranuka · Nonouti
 Tabiteuea · Nikunau
Banaba   Onotoa · Beru
(Ocean) Tamana · · Arorae

Te Aono N Kiribati
(Gilbert Group)

Howland (U.S.) ·
· Baker (U.S.)

Te Aono N Rawaki
(Phoenix Group)

McKean · Kanton · · Enderbury
 Birnie · · Rawaki
Nikumaroro   (Phoenix)
(Gardner) · Orono · · Manra
         (Hull)   (Sydney)

Kingman Reef (U.S.) ·
· Palmyra (U.S.)
 · Teraina
   (Washington)
  · Tabuaeran
    (Fanning)
       · Kiritimati
         (Christmas)

Northern Line Islands

Te Aono N Raina
(Line Islands)

Jarvis Island (U.S.) ·

Malden ·
       · Rawaki

Starbuck ·

Central Line Islands

Vostok ·

· Filippo Reef

Southern Line Islands

· Caroline
· Flint

Tokelau (N.Z.)

Cook Islands

0 500
kilometers

Kiribati and the United States: a spatial comparison

Northern Line Islands
460 km
3280 km
Phoenix Group
1750 km
Gilbert Group
470 km
4210 km
Central Line Islands
Southern Line Islands

0 500 1000
kilometers

Source: Lands and Survey Division, Bairiki, Tarawa, 1985.

KIRIBATI

Geography

Kiribati (pronounced Kiribas) is a country of 33 low-lying coral atolls in the middle of the Pacific Ocean. They comprise a total land area of 811 km^2 in a sea area of 5 million km^2. They are scattered from 4 degrees 43 minutes N to 11 degrees 25 minutes S latitude and 169 degrees 32 minutes E to 150 degrees 14 minutes W longitude. The capital is Bairiki on the island of Tarawa. Kiribati's neighbors are Nauru to the west, Tuvalu and Tokelau to the south, and Hawaii to the north.

Population

The population of Kiribati is 67,000 with a density of 83 per km^2. They are Micronesian, are identified as I-Kiribati, and speak Gilbertese and English. Thirty-three percent of the people live on Tarawa.

Politics

The islands of Kiribati were formerly the Gilbert Islands, administered as a British territory together with the Ellice Islands (now Tuvalu). They became an independent state in 1979. The government is a popular democracy with a president and a legislature.

Economy

Kiribati has an economy based on subsistence farming, copra, and fishing. Due to the nature of the low-lying coral atolls, agricultural diversification opportunities are limited. The GNP of Kiribati is $33 million (1989) with a GNP per capita of $471. Main exports are copra and fish.

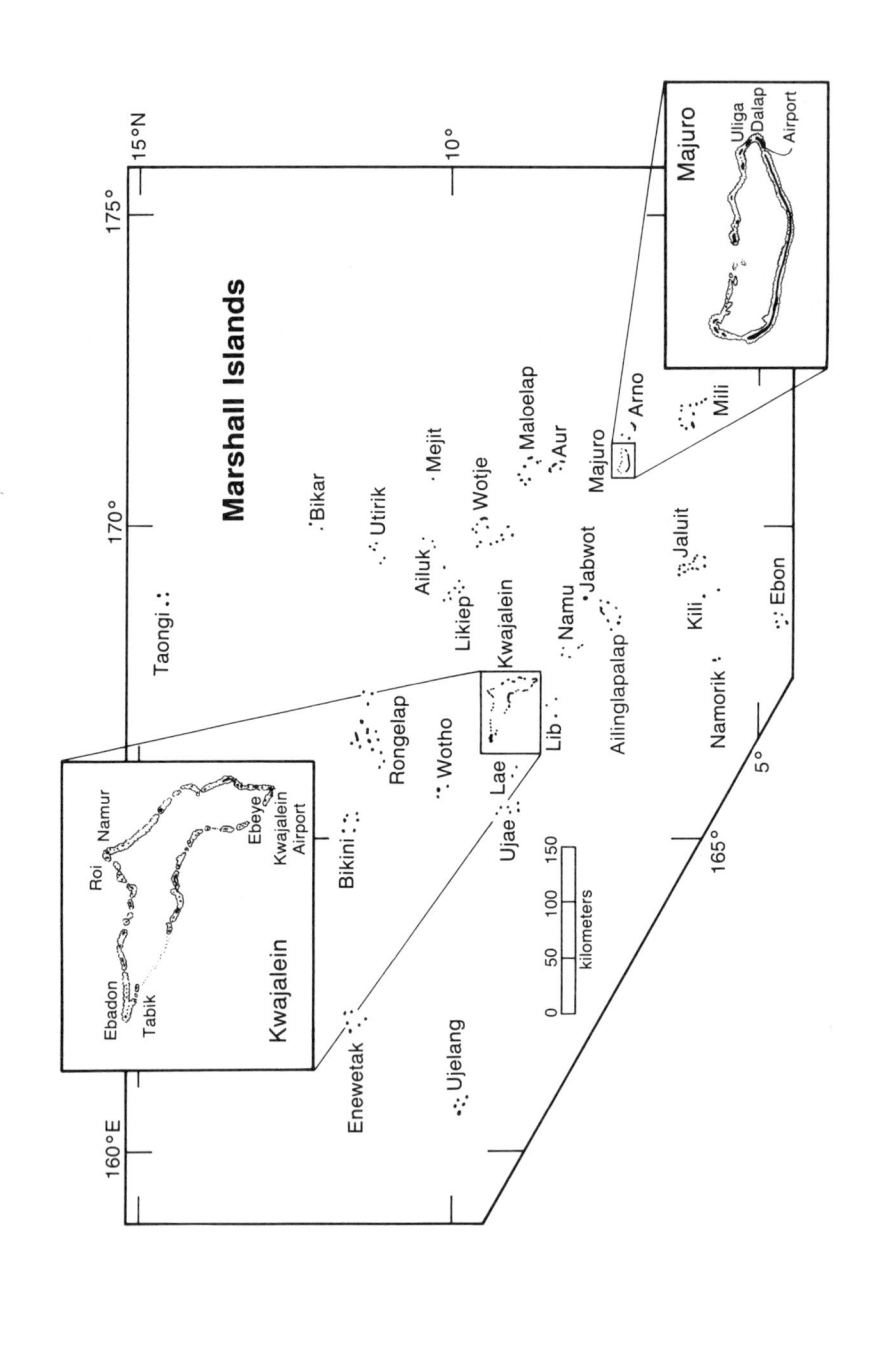

MARSHALL ISLANDS

Geography

The Marshall Islands are a series of 34 low-lying coral atolls compromising a land area of 171 km² in a sea area of around 2 million km². These islands are scattered between 5 and 15 degrees N latitude and 162 and 173 degrees E longitude. The largest island and capital is Majuro. The Marshall Islands' closest neighbors are FSM to the west, Nauru to the south, and Kiribati to the southeast.

Population

The Marshallese people are of Micronesian descent and speak Marshallese and English. The population of the Marshall Islands is about 44,000 with a density of 257 per km². Sixty-five percent of the islanders live on Majuro and on tiny Eyebe island in Kwajalein atoll.

Politics

The Republic of the Marshall Islands was formerly part of the United Nations Trust Territory of the Pacific Islands. It became self-governing in free association with the United States in 1986. The Marshall Islands are governed by a legislature and president.

Economy

The mainstays of the economy are subsistence farming, fishing, copra production, and U.S. military spending at Kwajalein Atoll. Per capita GNP is $1,317 (1984).

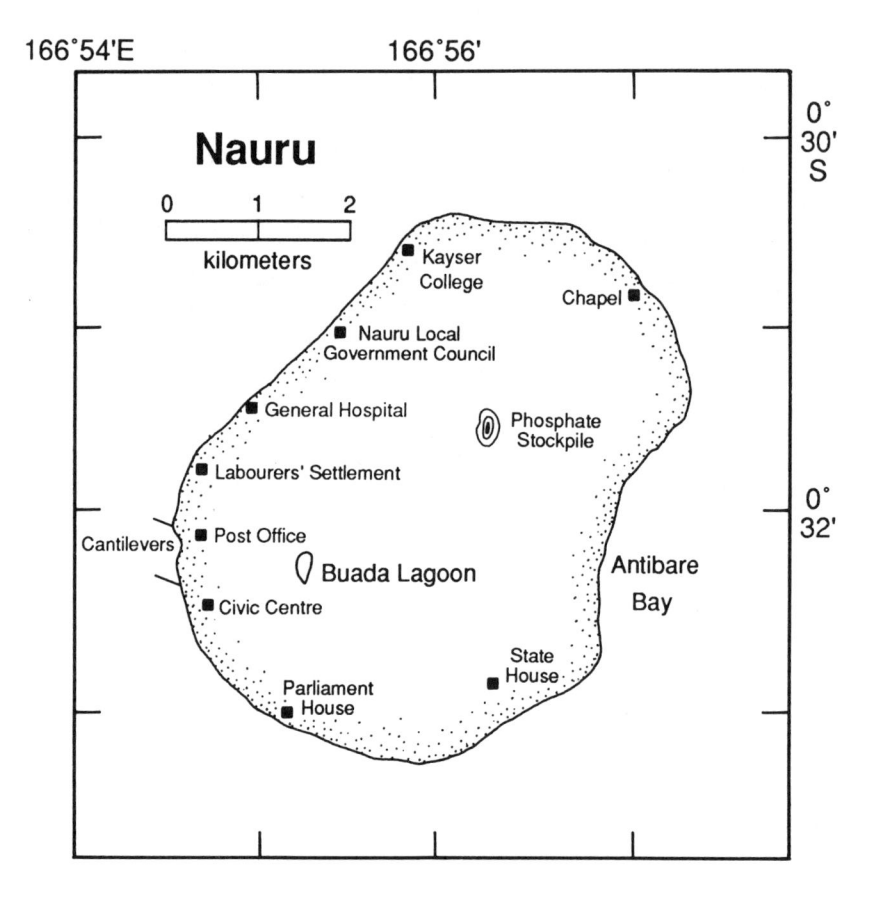

Nauru

0 1 2
kilometers

- Kayser College
- Chapel
- Nauru Local Government Council
- General Hospital
- Phosphate Stockpile
- Labourers' Settlement
- Cantilevers
- Post Office
- Buada Lagoon
- Antibare Bay
- Civic Centre
- State House
- Parliament House

166°54'E 166°56' 0°30'S 0°32'

NAURU

Geography

Nauru is a single uplifted coral atoll with a land area of 21 km². Its EEZ has an area of 320,000 km². Nauru is situated 41 km south of the equator at 166 degrees 56 minutes E longitude. The capital is Yaren. Nauru's closest neighbors are the Federated States of Micronesia and the Marshall Islands to the north, Kiribati to the east, and Solomon Islands to the south.

Population

Nauruans are Micronesians. The island of Nauru has a population of about 8,000 with a population density of 381 per km². Of this 8,000, about 5,000 are native Nauruans. The others are immigrant workers. The main languages are Nauruan and English.

Politics

Nauru was administered by Australia until independence in 1968. The Republic of Nauru has a democratic government headed by a president.

Economy

The main economic activity of Nauru is phosphate mining that gives Nauru the highest GNP per capita in the Pacific—$8,070 (1985). The GNP of Nauru is $186 million (1989), based almost entirely on phosphate mining. The phosphate will soon run out, and Nauru is investing its revenues in anticipation of that eventuality. A major national issue is reclamation of the mine area.

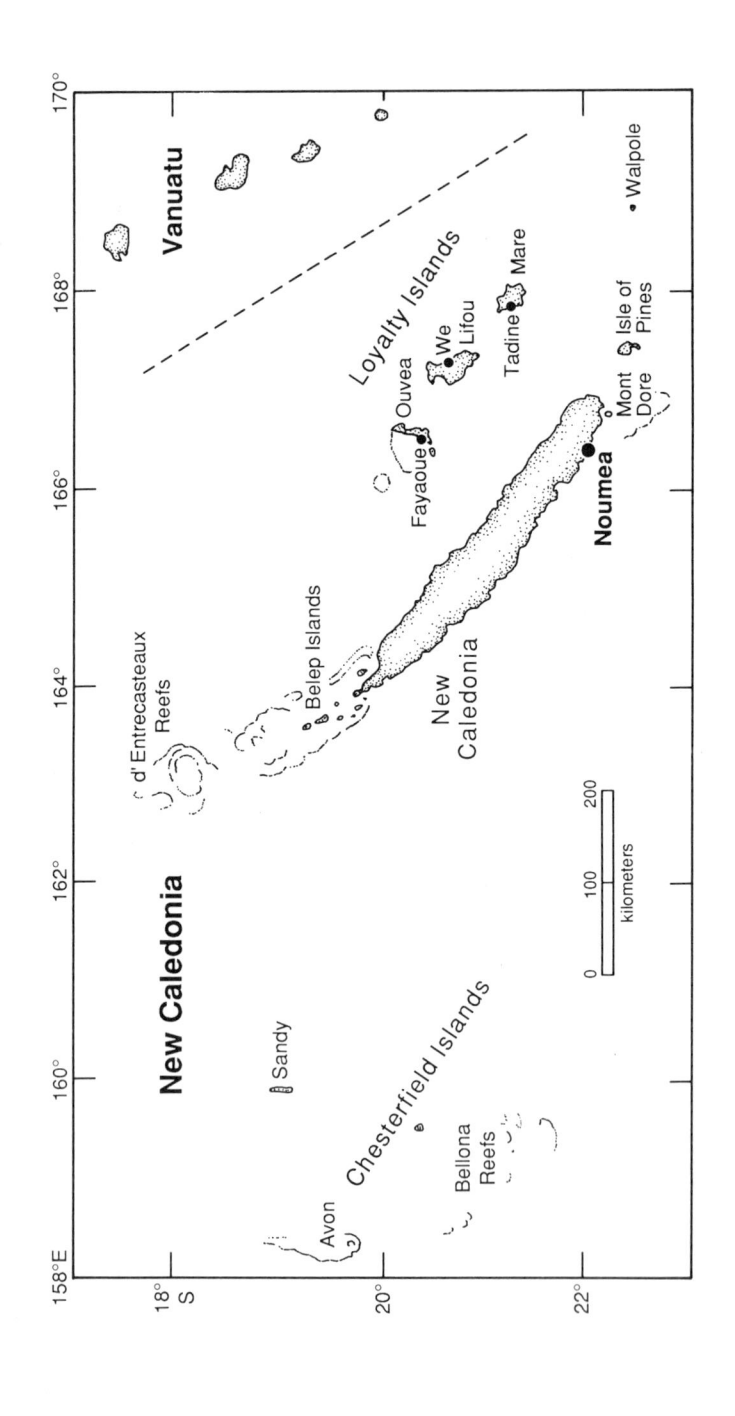

NEW CALEDONIA

Geography

New Caledonia consists of one large island, one smaller island, and the Loyalty and Huon island groups. The largest island is New Caledonia (known in France as La Grande Terre), where the capital of Noumea is located. Total land area is 19,103 km^2 and total sea area is 1,740,000 km^2. The islands lie between 19 and 23 degrees S latitude and between 163 and 168 degrees E longitude. New Caledonia's nearest neighbors are Vanuatu to the northeast and Australia to the southwest.

Population

The population of New Caledonia is 153,500 with a population density of 8 per km^2. About 43 percent of the total are indigenous Melanesians. Nickel industry development during the late 1960s stimulated immigration from France, North Africa, Vanuatu, Wallis, Tahiti, and the French Caribbean, which represent the majority of the population mix. All New Caledonians have full French citizenship. The official language is French, but about 30 Kanak dialects are spoken.

Politics

New Caledonia is an overseas territory of France. Control is vested in a high commissioner who is appointed by the French government. A 36-member Territorial Assembly is elected by popular vote. Two deputies, elected by universal suffrage, represent New Caledonia in the French National Assembly and one senator represents the territory in the French Senate. He is elected by an electoral college of representatives from the municipal councils and all members of the Territorial Assembly.

Economy

The economy of New Caledonia now centers around nickel production, but the islands have immense other mineral resources that also include iron, manganese, and cobalt. The only agricultural exports are coffee and copra. Tourism has become the second most important industry since 1981 when it was recognized as an economic development priority. GDP is $860 million and per capita GDP is $5,760 (1985 figures).

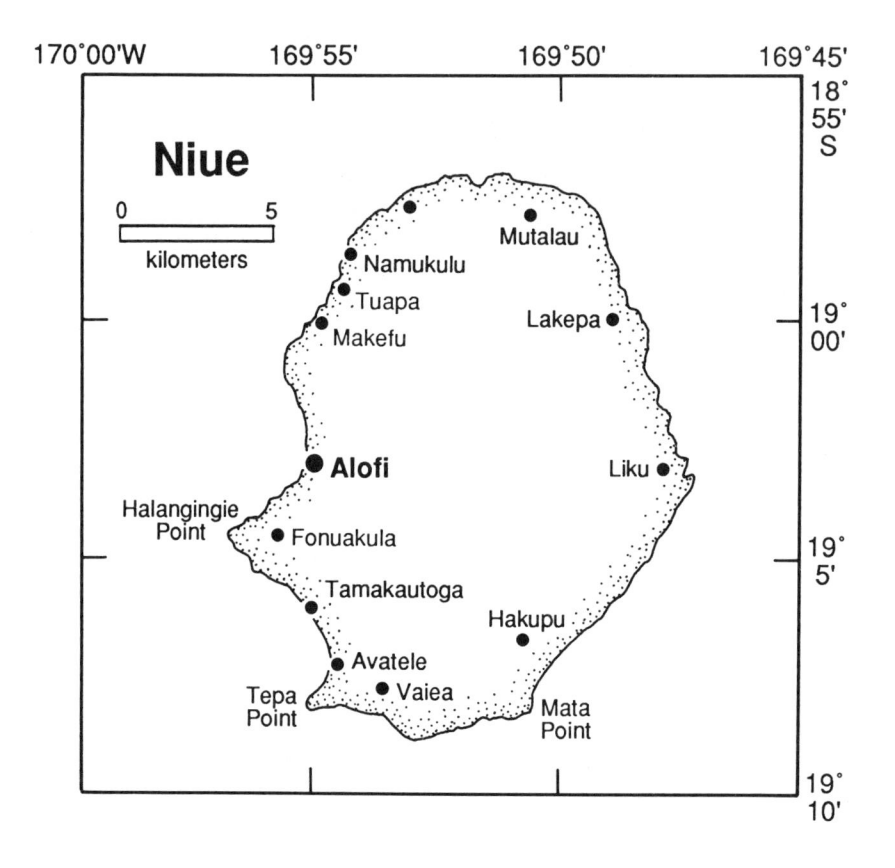

Niue

NIUE

Geography

Niue is a small uplifted coral atoll with an area of 258 km². Niue's EEZ is about 390,000 km². It is located at 19 degrees S latitude and 169 degrees W longitude. Its closest neighbors are Tonga to the west, Cook Islands to the east, and American Samoa to the north. The capital is Alofi.

Population

There are about 2,500 Niueans on Niue with a population density of 10 per km². Niueans are Polynesian. Both Niuean and English are spoken. A large number of Niueans migrate to New Zealand; as a result there are about three times as many Niueans in New Zealand as there are on Niue.

Politics

Niue was administered by New Zealand until it became self-governing in free association with New Zealand in 1974. Niue is a parliamentary democracy headed by a prime minister.

Economy

The GNP of Niue is $3 million (1985) with a GNP per capita of $1,080. Primary exports are fruit products (lime and passion fruit), root crops, coconut products, honey, and footballs.

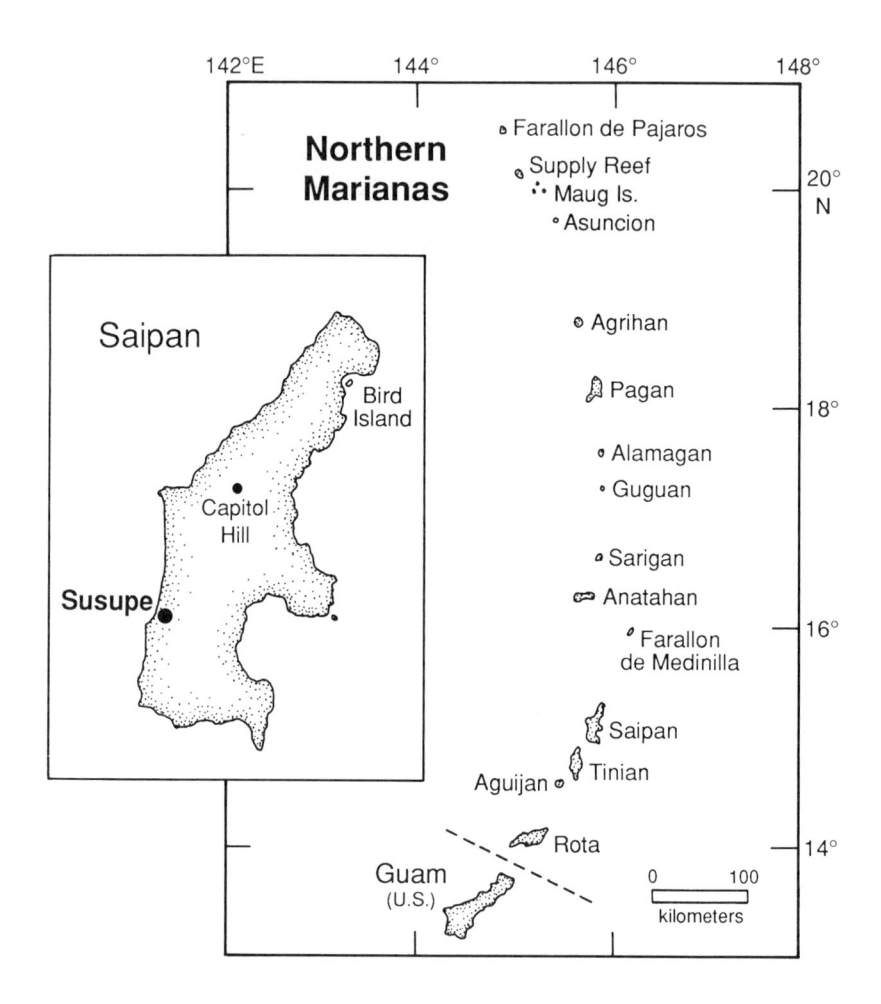

NORTHERN MARIANAS

Geography

The Northern Marianas contain 17 islands in the North Pacific running north to south for a distance of 543 km, from 20 degrees 33 minutes to 14 degrees 08 minutes N latitude all within 145 to 146 degrees E longitude. The main island is Saipan, where the administrative center is located. The total land area is 475 km² with a sea area of 777,000 km². The islands are mountainous "highlands" of either limestone or volcanic rock. The Marianas' closest neighbors are Guam and the Federated States of Micronesia to the south, and the Marshall Islands to the southeast.

Population

The total population is 20,600 with a density of 43 per km² centered on the island of Saipan. The population, once moved by the Spanish to Guam and the Caroline Islands, has great cultural and social diversity. The islanders are Micronesian, with the Chamorros making up the majority. Chamorro, Carolinian, and English are widely spoken.

Politics

The Northern Marianas is a self-governing Commonwealth in union with the United States under a covenant signed in 1975. The three branches of government consist of the executive, an elected governor and lieutenant governor; a bicameral legislature composed of a 9-member Senate and 14-member House of Representatives all elected by popular vote; and a judiciary.

Economy

Over half of the local budget is a direct U.S. subsidy. Tourism represents the major industry, but private business entrepreneurs continue to increase as the economic base develops to include construction, retailing, and service industries. GNP is $165 million and per capita GNP is $9,170 (1982 figures).

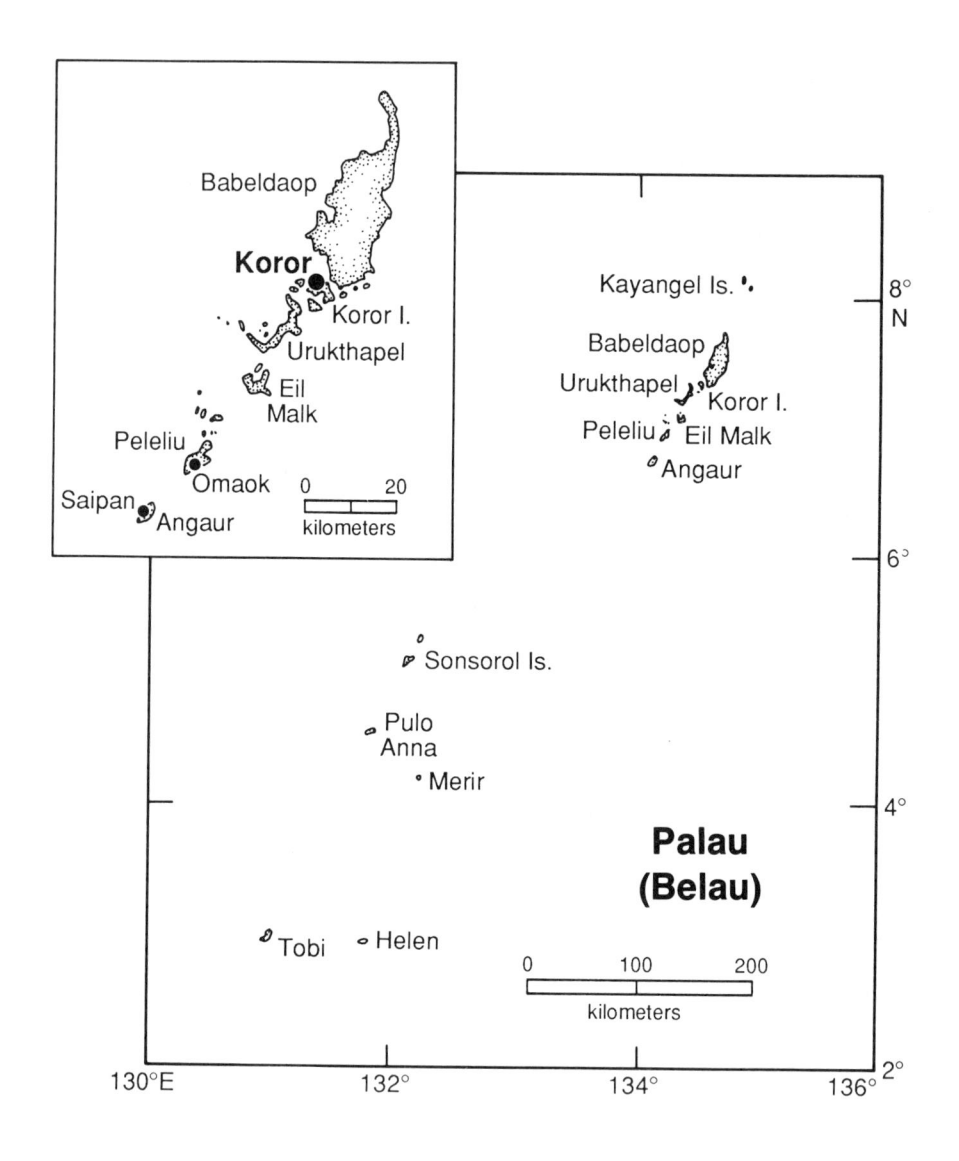

Palau (Belau)

Inset map

Babeldaop
Koror
Koror I.
Urukthapel
Eil Malk
Peleliu
Saipan
Omaok
Angaur

0   20
kilometers

Main map

Kayangel Is.
Babeldaop
Urukthapel
Koror I.
Peleliu
Eil Malk
Angaur

Sonsorol Is.
Pulo Anna
Merir

Tobi   Helen

0   100   200
kilometers

8° N
6°
4°
2°

130°E   132°   134°   136°

PALAU (BELAU)

Geography

Palau is a group of some 340 islands with a total land area of about 500 km^2 and a sea area of 629,000 km^2. The islands lie between 6 degrees 50 minutes and 8 degrees 15 minutes N latitude and 133 degrees 50 minutes and 134 degrees 45 minutes E longitude. The main group of four larger islands—Arakaseson, Koror, Babeldaop, and Malakal—are all volcanic; the remainder are raised coral limestone, with one atoll to the north. Palau's closest neighbors are the Federated States of Micronesia to the northeast and east, Indonesia to the south, Papua New Guinea to the southeast, and the Philippines to the west.

Population

The total population is 14,000 with a density of 28 per km^2. About 5,000 Palauans live elsewhere—mostly on Guam. Only eight of the islands in the group are permanently inhabited, and over half the population lives on the island of Koror where the administrative center is located. The islanders are Micronesian with considerable ethnic affinity to the people of the Federated States of Micronesia. English is widely spoken, as are a number of indigenous dialects of the Malayo-Polynesian language family.

Politics

The Republic of Palau was formed under a constitution in January 1981. A president and vice president are elected by popular vote. The executive branch is of a ministerial-type with the president choosing his cabinet. A bicameral legislature is composed of a House of Delegates made up of one delegate each from 16 states, and a Senate of 14 members. Although there have been seven referendums on a Compact of Free Association with the United States, these have failed to attain the two-thirds majority vote needed to resolve a conflict between U.S. nuclear defense policy and a non-nuclear provision in the Palauan constitution.

Economy

The economy of Palau is almost entirely based on grants from the U.S. government. There is a small fishing industry. Tourism is regarded as having great potential importance. GDP is $31.6 million and per capita GDP $2,257 (1986 figures).

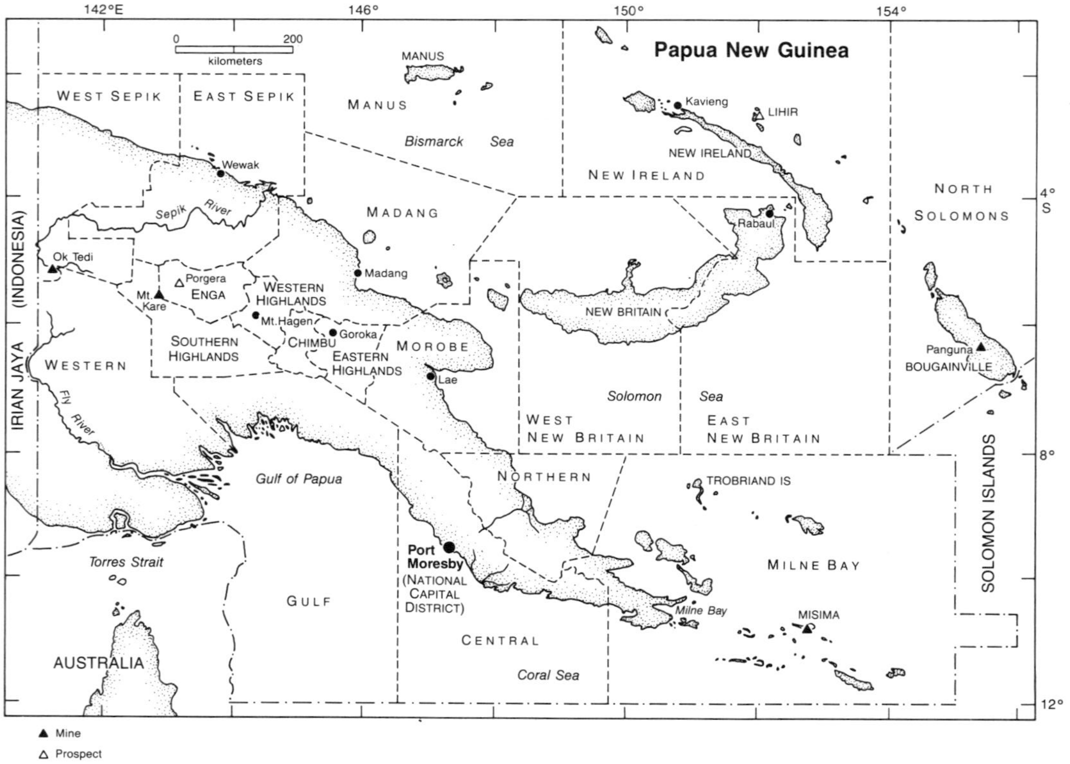
Papua New Guinea
142°E
146°
150°
154°
4° S
8°
12°
0
200
kilometers
WEST SEPIK
EAST SEPIK
MANUS
MANUS
Bismarck Sea
NEW IRELAND
NEW IRELAND
Kavieng
LIHIR
NORTH SOLOMONS
Wewak
Sepik River
MADANG
Madang
Rabaul
NEW BRITAIN
Ok Tedi
Porgera
ENGA
Mt. Kare
WESTERN HIGHLANDS
Mt. Hagen
Goroka
CHIMBU
EASTERN HIGHLANDS
MOROBE
SOUTHERN HIGHLANDS
WESTERN
Lae
Panguna
BOUGAINVILLE
IRIAN JAYA (INDONESIA)
Fly River
Solomon Sea
WEST NEW BRITAIN
EAST NEW BRITAIN
Gulf of Papua
NORTHERN
TROBRIAND IS
SOLOMON ISLANDS
Port Moresby
(NATIONAL CAPITAL DISTRICT)
MILNE BAY
Milne Bay
MISIMA
Torres Strait
GULF
CENTRAL
Coral Sea
AUSTRALIA
▲ Mine
△ Prospect

PAPUA NEW GUINEA

Geography

Papua New Guinea is the largest of the Pacific island states. It comprises a total land area of 461,690 km², located between 0 and 12 degrees S latitude and 141 and 160 degrees E longitude. This broad range encompasses an EEZ of 3,108,000 km². The largest part of Papua New Guinea is situated on the eastern half of the island of New Guinea. The capital of Port Moresby is located on the southern coast of this island. Other major islands are New Britain, New Ireland, Bougainville, and Manus. These are large continental islands with rugged terrain. There are also many smaller islands. Papua New Guinea's nearest neighbors are Indonesia to the west, with which it shares a land border (Irian Jaya), and Australia to the south. Solomon Islands are to the east and the Federated States of Micronesia and Palau are to the north.

Population

The population of Papua New Guinea is 3.5 million. With the large land mass, the population density is only 7.6 per km². Many villages are isolated from each other. The southern coast of New Guinea is separated from the populous central and northern parts of the country by rugged terrain. There are about 700 language and cultural groups in this Melanesian country. In addition, three languages are spoken by many groups. These are Tokpisin (pidgin), Hiri Motu, and English.

Politics

Papua New Guinea was administered by Australia from World War I until independence in 1975. The country is divided into 19 administrative provinces and the National Capital District. The form of government is a parliamentary democracy headed by a prime minister.

Economy

Papua New Guinea has a GNP of $2,823 million (1989) and a GNP per capita of $820. The mainstays of the economy are subsistence and plantation agriculture, fisheries, and mining. Major exports are copper, gold, fish products, copra products, coffee, cocoa, timber, and tea.

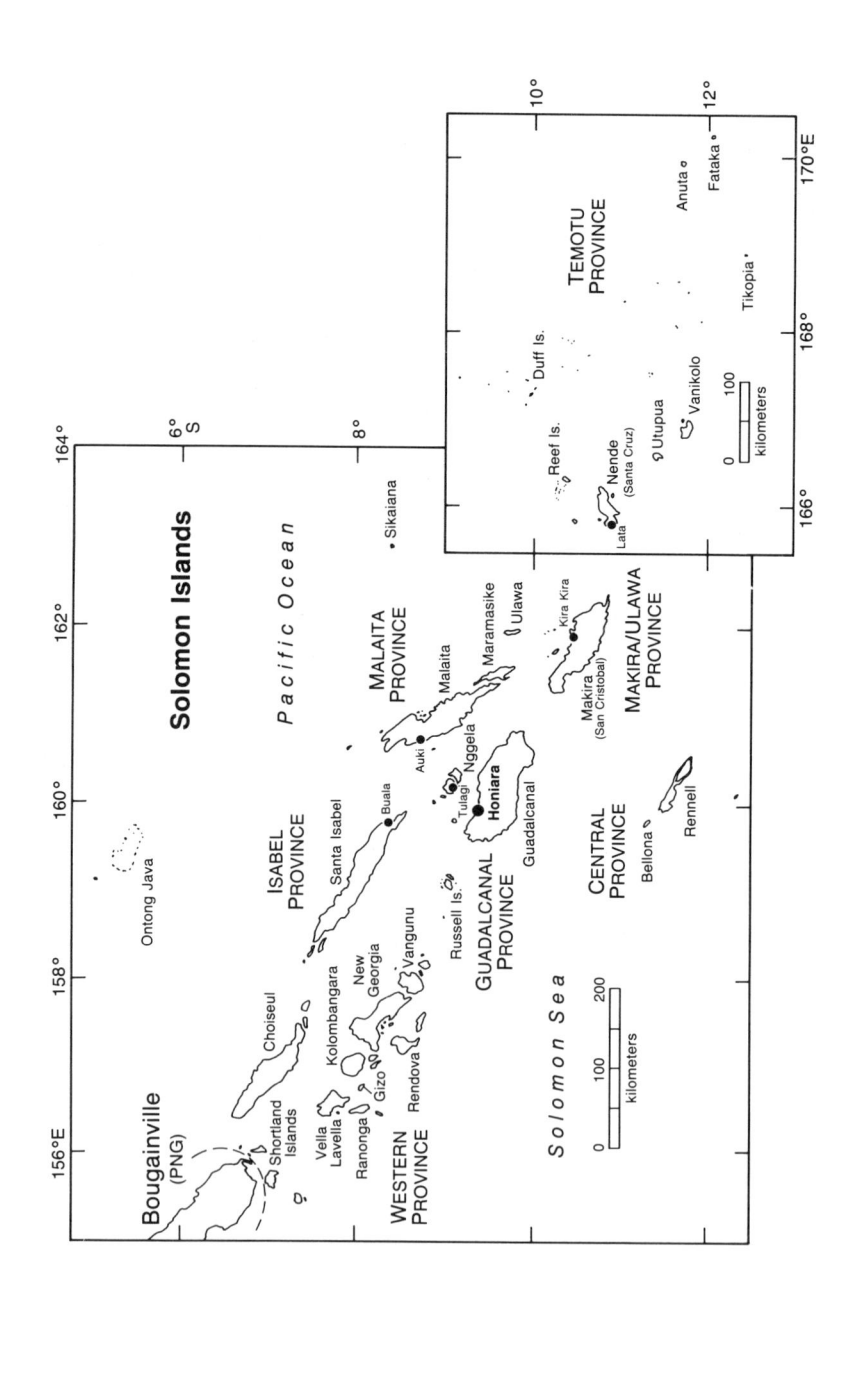

SOLOMON ISLANDS

Geography

Solomon Islands is a chain of six large islands and many smaller islands located between 5 and 12 degrees S latitude and 155 and 170 degrees E longitude. They comprise a land area of 29,785 km^2 extending over 600,000 km^2 of sea. The major urban center and capital is Honiara located on the island of Guadalcanal. Solomon Islands' closest neighbors are Papua New Guinea to the west and Vanuatu to the southeast.

Population

Solomon Islanders are predominantly Melanesians with about 90 different language and ethnic groups; there are small numbers of Polynesians and Europeans. The total population is about 286,000 with a density of 10 per km^2. The major lingua franca is pidgin, with English being the official language.

Politics

Solomon Islands was a British colonial possession. The islands were the scene of major fighting during World War II, and became independent in 1978. The government of Solomon Islands is a parliamentary democracy.

Economy

The GNP of Solomon Islands is $133 million (1989), with a GNP per capita of $410. Solomon Islands' economy is based mainly on subsistence agriculture. The major exports are fish products, timber, palm oil and copra, cocoa, and some gold.

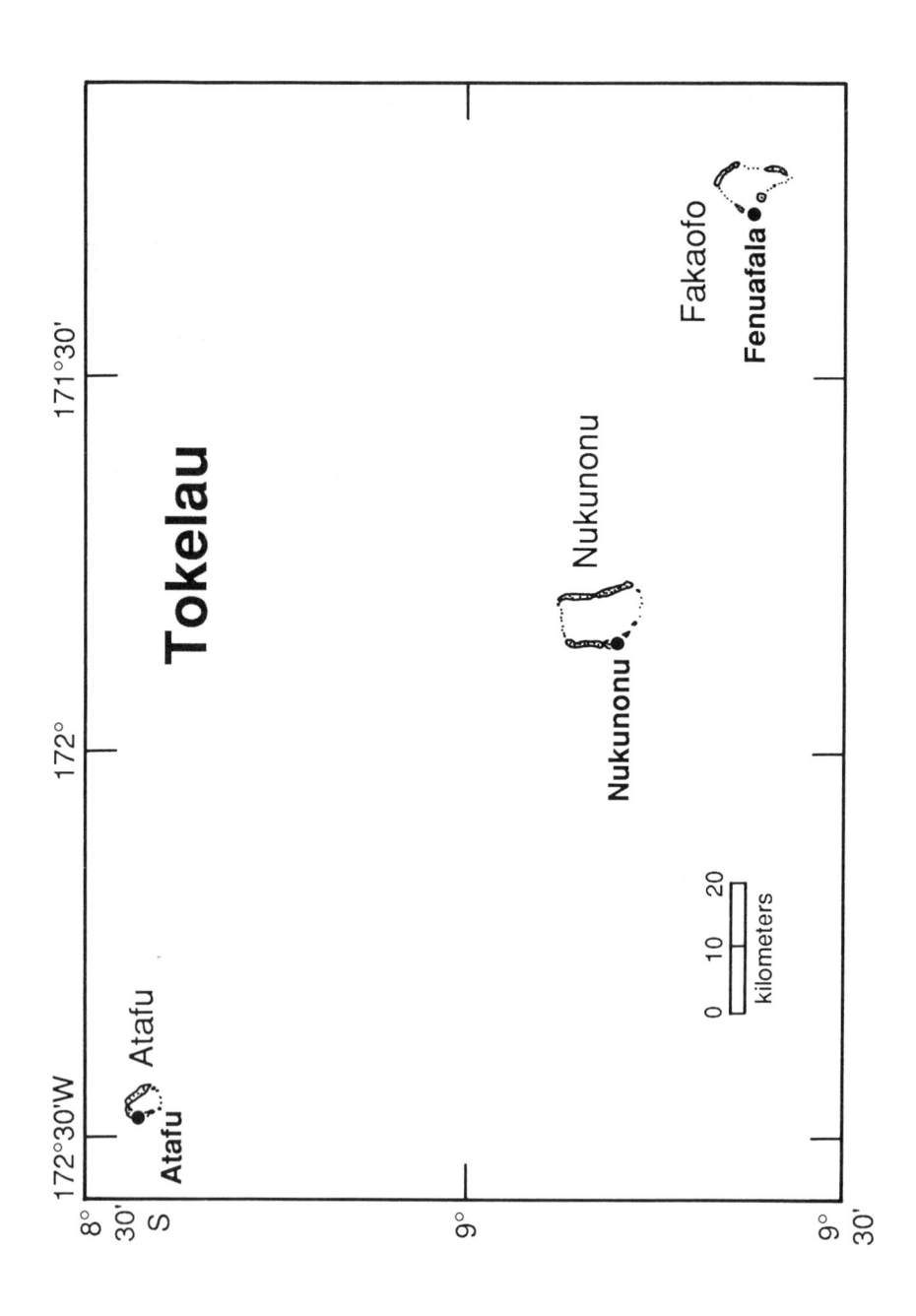

Tokelau

TOKELAU

Geography

Tokelau consists of three atolls—Atafu, Nukunonu, and Fakaofu—located between 8 and 10 degrees S latitude and 171 and 173 degrees W longitude. Each atoll has a number of reef-bound islets around a lagoon. Total dry-land area is 12.2 km², with 165 km² of enclosed lagoon area and 290,000 km² of territorial sea. Tokelau's nearest neighbors are Kiribati to the north, Tuvalu to the west, and Western Samoa and American Samoa to the south.

Population

The population of Tokelau is about 1,600 with a population density of about 131 per km². The people are Polynesian and have family, linguistic, and cultural links with Western Samoa due to the New Zealand government's administration of Tokelau from Apia since 1925. Tokelauans are British subjects and New Zealand citizens. Their language is similar to Samoan and Tuvaluan; English is sometimes spoken and is taught as a second language.

Politics

Tokelau is a non-self-governing territory administered by an administrator of Tokelau who is responsible to the New Zealand Ministry of Foreign Affairs through the Office for Tokelau Affairs. Powers of the administrator are delegated to an official secretary in Apia, Western Samoa. Each atoll has its own administrative center consisting of a commissioner or headman, village mayor, and village clerk who oversee day-to-day administration on each island, but the dominant village political body is the Council of Elders.

Economy

Tokelau's economy is based mainly on resources from the sea, and coconut and pandanus palms. Shortage of natural resources has been the major factor encouraging migration to Western Samoa and New Zealand. GDP is $1 million and per capita GDP is $670 (1983 figures).

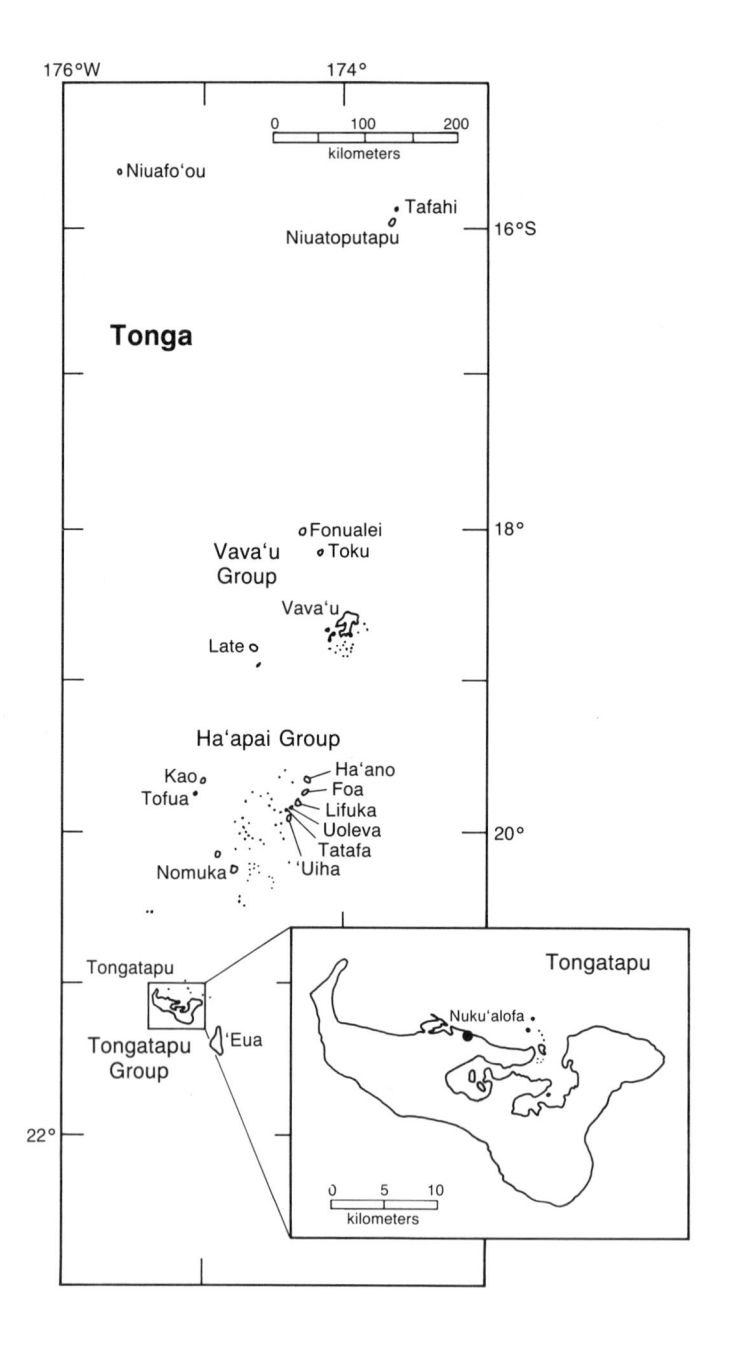

TONGA

Geography

The Kingdom of Tonga is located between 15 degrees and 23 degrees 30 minutes S latitude and 173 and 177 degrees W longitude. Tonga's closest neighbors are Fiji to the northwest, American Samoa and Western Samoa to the north, and Niue and Cook Islands to the east. Tonga comprises three main island groups (Tongatapu, Ha'apai, and Vava'u) that are mainly coral atolls with some volcanic islands. There are some 150 islands, of which 36 are inhabited. These islands have a land area of 697 km^2 with a sea area of 699,000 km^2. The capital, Nuku'alofa, is located on the southerly island of Tongatapu.

Population

Tongans are a Polynesian people with their own language. They number about 96,000 located mostly on the island of Tongatapu. The population density of Tonga is 138 per km^2. Both Tongan and English are spoken. There is a large number of Tongans living in New Zealand and the United States.

Politics

Tonga is a constitutional monarchy dating back to its first constitution in 1875 established by King Tupou I. Tonga was a protectorate of Great Britain until 1970 when it gained full control of its affairs. The executive and legislative functions are vested in the king, the prime minister, and parliament.

Economy

The GNP of Tonga is $78 million (1989) with a GNP per capita of $750. Most Tongans are involved in subsistence agriculture. The other main economic activities of Tonga are tourism, coconut products, bananas, vanilla, fish, squash, and some light manufacturing.

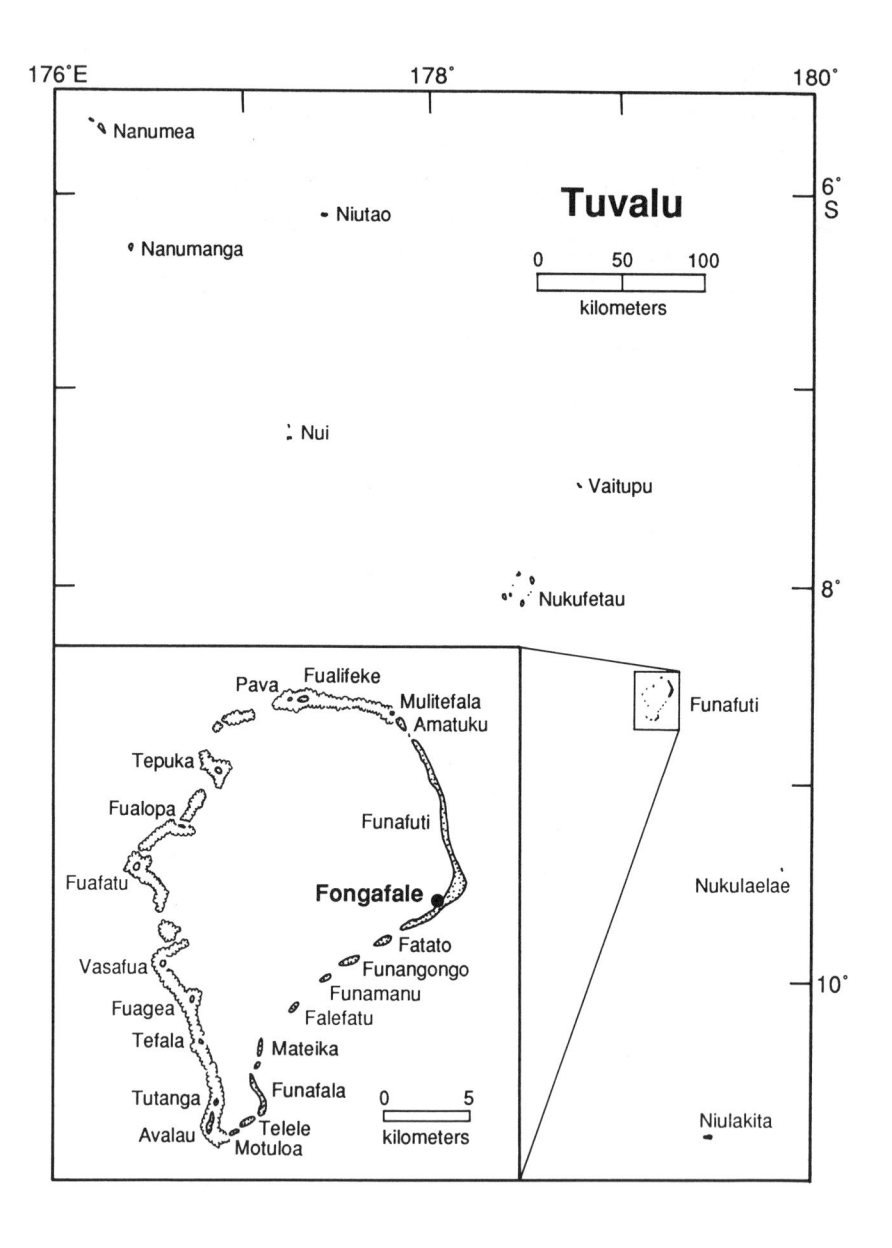

TUVALU

Geography

Tuvalu is a chain of nine low-lying coral atolls located between 5 and 10 degrees S latitude and 176 and 179 degrees E longitude. These atolls rise only a few feet above sea level and comprise a land area of only 26 km^2 in an ocean area of 906,000 km^2. The main island and capital is Funafuti. Tuvalu's closest neighbors are Kiribati to the north, Tokelau to the east, Fiji and Wallis and Futuna to the southwest, and Western Samoa and American Samoa to the southeast.

Population

Tuvaluans are Polynesian. They speak Tuvaluan, which is closely related to Samoan, and also English. There are 9,000 inhabitants with a population density of 346 per km^2. Most live on Funafuti.

Politics

Tuvalu was once a part of the British territory of Gilbert and Ellice Islands. The Gilbert Islands became part of Kiribati, and the Ellice Islands became the independent state of Tuvalu in 1978. Tuvalu is a parliamentary democracy.

Economy

Tuvaluans are engaged mainly in subsistence agriculture and fishing. The GNP is $4 million (1989) with a per capita income of $500. The only agriculture that the limited soil allows is copra production. There is also some export of fish.

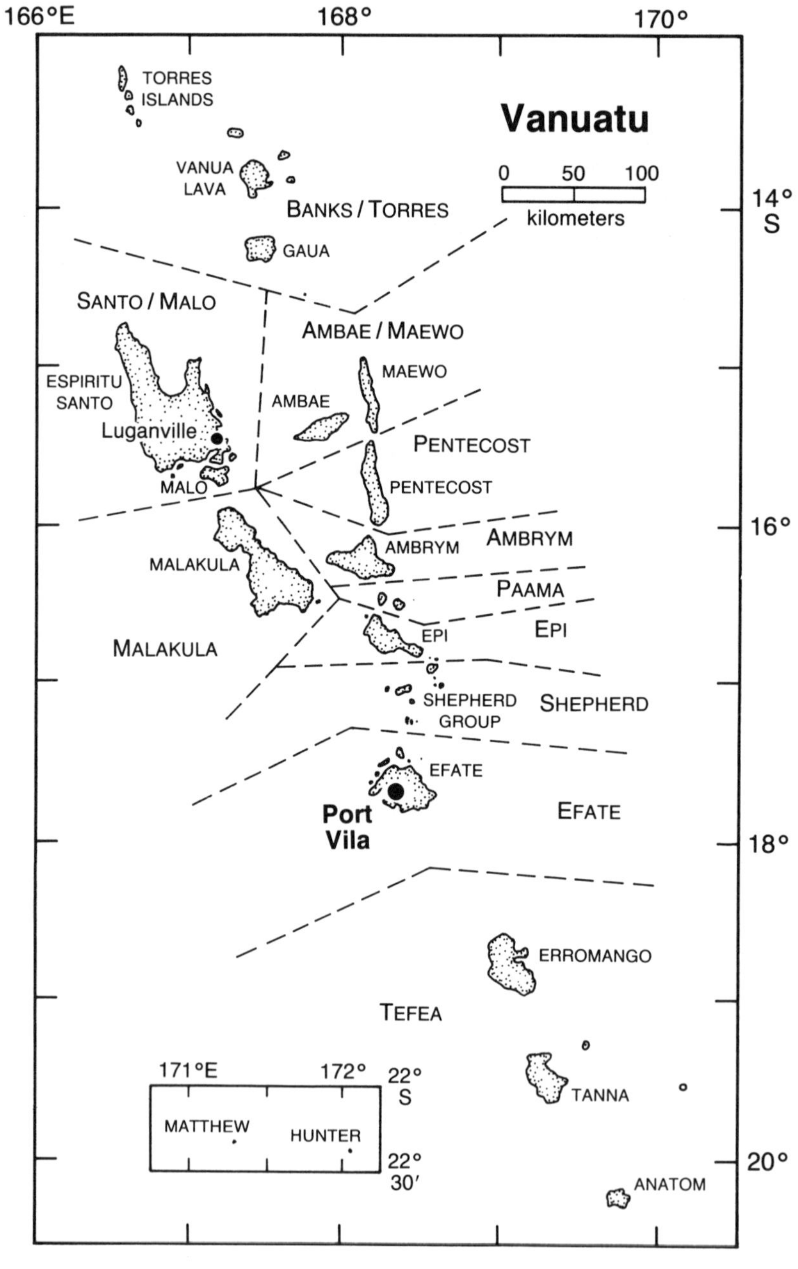
166°E
168°
170°
Vanuatu
0
50
100
kilometers
14°
S
16°
18°
20°
TORRES
ISLANDS
VANUA
LAVA
BANKS / TORRES
GAUA
SANTO / MALO
AMBAE / MAEWO
MAEWO
ESPIRITU
SANTO
AMBAE
Luganville
PENTECOST
MALO
PENTECOST
AMBRYM
MALAKULA
AMBRYM
PAAMA
EPI
EPI
MALAKULA
SHEPHERD
GROUP
SHEPHERD
EFATE
Port
Vila
EFATE
ERROMANGO
TEFEA
171°E
172°
22°
S
MATTHEW
HUNTER
22°
30′
TANNA
ANATOM

VANUATU

Geography

Vanuatu is made up of about 80 islands located from 12 to 21 degrees S latitude and 166 to 171 degrees E longitude. They comprise a land area of 11,880 km² with an EEZ of 686,000 km². Vanuatu's islands are a combination of large high islands and small coral atolls. Their nearest neighbors are Fiji to the east, Solomon Islands to the north, and New Caledonia to the south. The capital is Port Vila on the island of Efate.

Population

The people of Vanuatu are referred to as ni-Vanuatu and are a Melanesian people with 100 different ethnic and language groups. There are about 150,000 people in Vanuatu with a density of 13 per km². English, French, and Bislama (Vanuatu Pidgin) are widely spoken.

Politics

In the colonial period, Vanuatu was administered jointly by Great Britain and France. Vanuatu gained independence in 1980. It is a parliamentary democracy headed by a prime minister.

Economy

The GNP of Vanuatu is $87 million (1989) with a per capita income of $568. The majority of the people live on subsistence agriculture. Major economic activities are tourism, copra production, cocoa, coffee, timber, fishing, and off-shore banking.

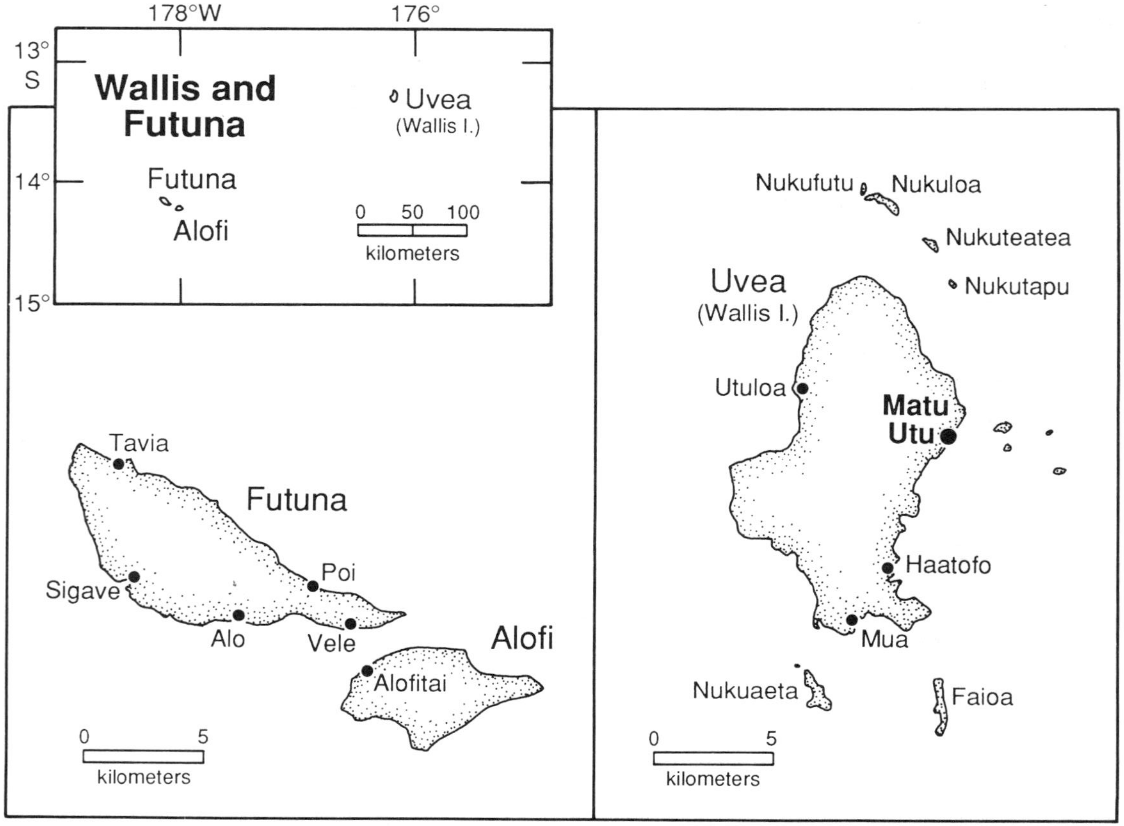
178°W
176°
13°
S
14°
15°
Wallis and
Futuna
Uvea
(Wallis I.)
Futuna
Alofi
0 50 100
kilometers
Tavia
Futuna
Poi
Sigave
Alo
Vele
Alofi
Alofitai
0 5
kilometers
Nukufutu
Nukuloa
Nukuteatea
Nukutapu
Uvea
(Wallis I.)
Utuloa
Matu
Utu
Haatofo
Mua
Nukuaeta
Faioa
0 5
kilometers

Profiles

WALLIS & FUTUNA

Geography

Wallis and Futuna consists of two separate islands about 200 km apart, extending from 13 degrees 20 minutes to 14 degrees 21 minutes S latitude and from 176 degrees 10 minutes to 178 degrees 10 minutes W longitude. The capital Mata Utu is located on Wallis Island. The islands are of volcanic origin surrounded by reefs and cover a land area of 255 km^2 and 300,000 km^2 of sea area. Wallis and Futuna's nearest neighbors are Fiji to the southwest, Tuvalu to the northwest, and Western Samoa and American Samoa to the west.

Population

The population of Wallis and Futuna is 14,700 with a density of 58 per km^2, with the majority of islanders living on Wallis Island. The islanders are Polynesian and have French nationality, with French being the official language. The local languages belong to the Malayo-Polynesian family, but the language spoken on Futuna, which has many linguistic properties of Samoan, is distinct from the Wallisian language, which is more closely related to Tongan.

Politics

Wallis and Futuna is an overseas territory of France. The territory is divided into three districts corresponding to the three kingdoms of Wallis, Alo (Futuna), and Sigave (Futuna). A French administrator is the head of the territory, and he is ex-officio the president of the Territorial Council, which includes a king from each of the districts and another three members appointed by himself with the approval of the Territorial Assembly. The assembly consists of 20 members (13 from Wallis and 7 from Futuna) elected by popular vote. Wallis and Futuna is represented in Paris in the National Assembly by a deputy elected by popular vote, and a senator elected to the French Senate by members of the Territorial Assembly based on a simple majority vote.

Economy

Wallis and Futuna has a subsistence economy heavily funded by the French government. The main sources of cash income are government work, and funds sent home by relatives working in New Caledonia. Agricultural production meets local consumption needs, but there is little prospect for agricultural development because of a shortage of fertile soil and an inherited land-tenure system. Total GDP is $7.9 million (estimate for 1985).

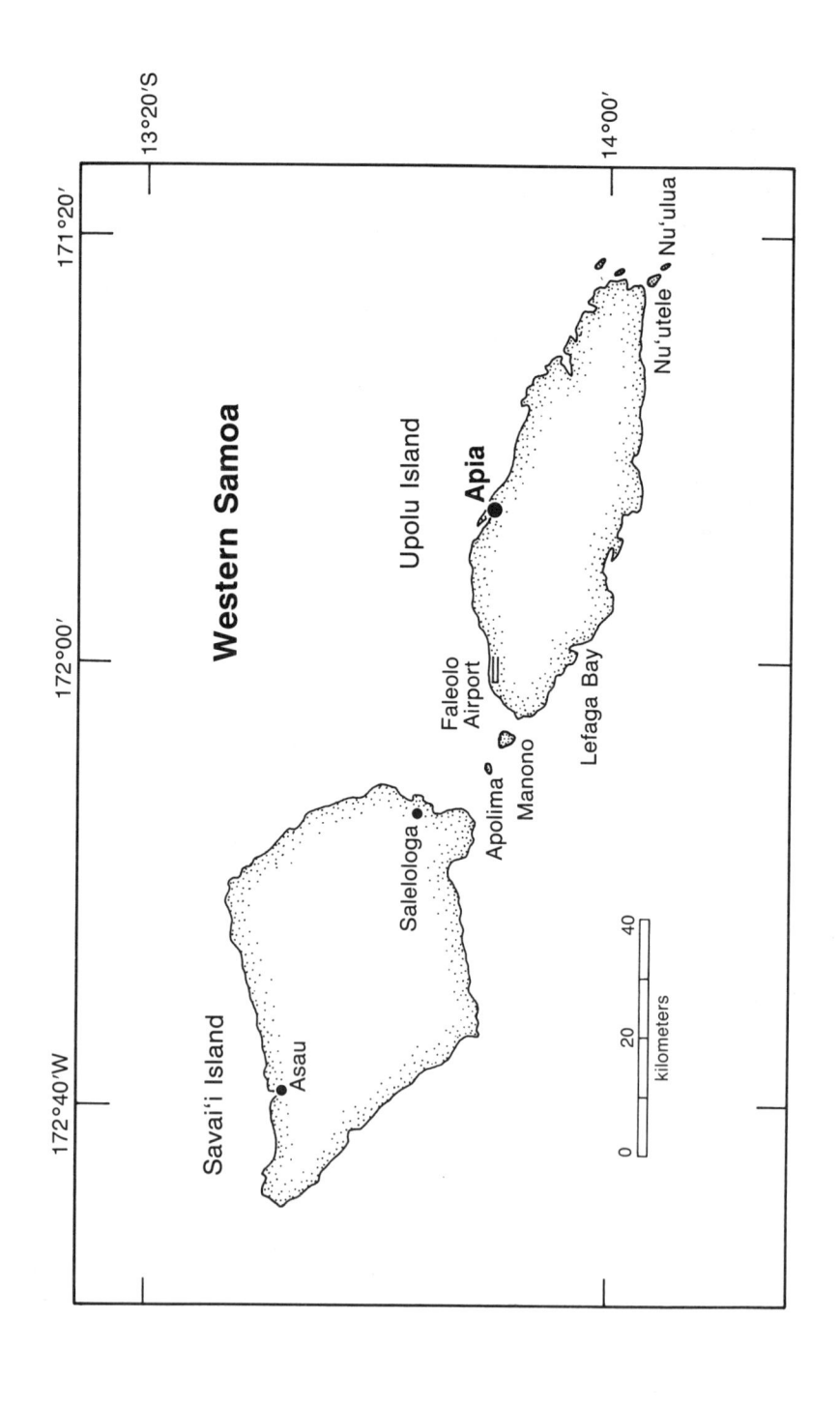

WESTERN SAMOA

Geography

Western Samoa is made up of two large and two small inhabited islands. They are located between 13 and 15 degrees S latitude and 168 and 173 degrees W longitude. The land area of Western Samoa is about 2,934 km^2 with an EEZ of 122,000 km^2. The capital is Apia, located on the island of Upolu. Western Samoa's neighbors are Fiji in the west, Tonga to the south, Tuvalu and Tokelau to the north, and American Samoa to the east. Western Samoa's main islands are large volcanic islands.

Population

The population of Western Samoa is 170,000. The population density is 58 per km^2. Western Samoans live mainly on the island of Upolu and around the capital Apia. Western Samoans are Polynesian and speak both the Samoan and English languages. While Western Samoa has a high birth rate, the growth rate of the resident population is stable due to migration to New Zealand and the United States.

Politics

Western Samoa was formerly a German colony. It became a League of Nations mandate and later a UN trust territory administered by New Zealand. In 1962 Western Samoa became the first country in the Pacific islands to regain full independence. It has a parliamentary democracy based on the English model and traditional culture.

Economy

The GNP of Western Samoa is $98 million (1989) with a per capita income of $539. Most of the population is engaged in subsistence agriculture. There is some light manufacturing and tourism. Remittances from family members overseas contribute a large part of foreign exchange earnings. The primary exports are copra, timber, cocoa, bananas, and taro.

SOURCES

Countries of the World and Their Leaders Yearbook 1982, Vol. 1 and 2. Detroit: Gale Research Company, 1982.

The Far East and Australasia 1991, 22nd edition. London: Europa Publications Limited, 1990.

Douglas, Norman and Ngaire, editors. *Pacific Islands Yearbook*, 16th edition. North Ryde, NSW, Australia: Angus & Robertson Publishers, 1989.

Stanley, David. *South Pacific Handbook*, 3rd edition. Chico, California: Moon Publications, 1986.

APPENDIX 2
Notes on the Leading Intergovernmental Regional Organizations in the Pacific Island Region

This section provides supplementary information on the South Pacific Commission (SPC) as well as information on other regional and subregional organizations mentioned but not described in the text. Apart from the SPC, the regional organizations and arrangements described are

- South Pacific Forum Secretariat
- Pacific Forum Line (PFL)
- Forum Fisheries Agency (FFA)
- South Pacific Trade Commission (SPTC)
- South Pacific Applied Geoscience Commission (SOPAC)
- South Pacific Regional Environment Program (SPREP)
- Pacific Islands Development Program (PIDP)

South Pacific Commission (SPC)

The SPC consists of a secretariat, headed by a secretary-general who is responsible to the South Pacific Conference as the supreme policy-making body. The conference, which meets annually, exercises final authority over the SPC's work program, approves the annual budget, and appoints the principal officers including the secretary-general. The conference is assisted by a committee—the Committee of Participating Governments and Administrations (CPGA)—in formulating a work program and in attending to administrative matters. The CPGA meets twice a year.

Headquartered in Noumea, the SPC also operates a small office in Sydney and a community training center for women in Suva (the Community Education Training Centre or CETC). All told, the SPC employs approximately 70 technical specialists and 80 support staff. Its budget, both core and extra budgetary, amounts to around $7.8 million.

The SPC provides island countries with technical, consultative, and advisory assistance in the spheres of development specified in the Canberra Agreement. Emphasis is given to practical, grassroots approaches that are effective in raising the quality of life of village communities. Activities are expected to yield tangible and fairly immediate benefits to the local people. Such an approach contrasts strongly with the SPC's initial orientations that focused on research, fact-finding, and technical studies whose results were made available to the colonial powers to assist them in improving the social and economic life of their respective island territory.

Administratively, the SPC's work program is organized under the following headings: food and materials, marine resources, rural management and technology, community services, socioeconomic services, information services, and organization of regional consultations. Many of the SPC's project activities have been particularly well received by island countries—for example, improving potable water, collecting data on major diseases, promoting more efficient agricultural and fishing techniques, collecting and disseminating socioeconomic statistical indicators, and training. Some of these activities complement the work carried out by other regional (and international) bodies, noteworthy examples being surveys of regional billfish and tuna resources, and health and training services.

The evolution of the SPC to what it is today has been marked by considerable controversy, often involving direct confrontation between the representatives of island countries and the metropolitan powers. Island leaders baulked under the so-called no politics rule, and they felt increasingly frustrated by an organization that was unabashedly colonial in structure and tightly controlled by the metropolitan powers. These frustrations became increasingly evident from the 1960s as the island leaders became more assertive and as the process of decolonization accelerated. The no-politics rule still applies, but as a result of persistent pressure from island leaders—the most celebrated being the "rebellion" of 1965—the colonial obstructions to meaningful island participation in SPC have now been removed to the point where all member countries are represented on the basis of equality.[1] The series of measures that led to this state of affairs included the abolition of an archaic plural

---

[1] This rebellion occurred at the Sixth South Pacific Conference in Lae in 1965, where representatives of island countries—led by Ratu Mara of Fiji—demanded that Pacific island countries be allowed to play a more active role in the SPC, including making financial contributions. At that time only one island state, Western Samoa, was a full member of SPC—as one of the so-called participating governments.

voting system (1976) that favored the metropolitan countries; the broadening of membership qualifications (1978) to allow both independent countries and those who enjoyed self-government "in free association" with a fully independent government to become full members; and the establishment of the CPGA in place of two other committees: the Committee of Representatives of Participating Governments and the Planning and Evaluation Committee. The latter reform meant that all members of SPC, irrespective of political status, could enjoy an equal voice and voting power in the CPGA as they did in the South Pacific Conference.

South Pacific Forum Secretariat

The present membership of the Forum Secretariat is the same as that of the South Pacific Forum. The Forum Secretariat comprises two bodies: a Senior Officials Budget Committee and a permanent secretariat. The committee, comprising senior officials and, in some cases, ministers, meets once a year and is responsible for reviewing the Forum Secretariat's work program and budget. The Secretariat is headed by a secretary-general who reports to the Forum through the committee noted above. The secretary-general is assisted by two directors: Director of Programmes and Director of Services.

The Forum Secretariat's work program falls into several broad categories: trade and investment, transportation (civil aviation and maritime divisions), telecommunications, economic services, and energy. Among past achievements have been the coordination of studies and meetings leading to the establishment of the PFL, FFA, SPARTECA, and the Trade Commission Office in Sydney. Other major technical studies conducted under Forum Secretariat auspices include those on the industrial potential of member countries, the scope for regional harmonization of industrial incentives, bulk purchasing opportunities, and the potential for increased trade with Japan and the United States.

The Forum Secretariat is involved in several major regional projects within the general areas noted above. Recent initiatives include a South-Pacific Maritime Development Program designed to strengthen national infrastructural facilities and training efforts in the area of shipping; a South Pacific Telecommunications Program to improve telecommunication facilities, especially in smaller countries; and a Smaller Island Program aimed at meeting the special development needs of the small islands. Additionally, the Secretariat continues to be active in projects concerned with energy (especially conservation measures), tourism development, handicrafts, and marketing.

The Forum Secretariat's servicing roles are numerous. They include acting as secretariat for the Ministerial Council on Regional Civil

Aviation and its associated Advisory Committee and for the Managerial Group associated with the South Pacific Telecommunication Program. The Forum Secretariat also organizes meetings of the South Pacific Regional Shipping Council on Pacific Forum Line matters, facilitates meetings of the Association of South Pacific Airlines, and assists the eight Pacific members of the African, Caribbean, Pacific group (ACP) of countries associated with the European Economic Community (EEC) in negotiations over aid under the Lome Convention (the Secretariat is the regional authorizing agency for disbursal of aid under this scheme). Meetings on regional economic issues and trade are also serviced by the Secretariat.

Several organizations under the South Pacific Forum umbrella, including the Forum Fisheries Agency (FFA) and the Trade Commission and Shipping Council, report to the Forum through the Forum Secretariat. The secretary-general (or his representative) also chairs meetings of the SPREP Coordinating Committee. Under a Forum directive, the secretary-general also conducts liaison with ASEAN.

Other notable forms of assistance rendered by the Forum Secretariat include advisory assistance on natural disasters, training under a fellowship scheme, and expert services drawn from within the region.

Pacific Forum Line (PFL)

The PFL was founded in 1977 as a vehicle for regional cooperation in shipping—a vital service for Pacific island countries heavily dependent on trade and traditionally disadvantaged by fluctuating (and high) freight rates and sporadic services. Originally based on the "pooling" principle whereby ships are chartered rather than owned outright, PFL emerged as essentially a compromise, designed to keep to an absolute minimum the level of financial commitment expected from individual members. Also, for some members, such a compromise arrangement was consistent with their perception of an appropriate level of regional cooperation. Such a shipping venture would promote economic development in the region by acting as a mechanism for exercising some control over shipping developments, stabilizing freight rates and, at least in some degree, attending to the needs of the small island countries situated away from the trunk routes.

As a private company wholly owned by nine members of the South Pacific Forum, PFL presently operates three modern container vessels under charter—one each from New Zealand, Tonga, and Western Samoa.[2] (A smaller break bulk vessel is chartered from the government

---

2 The shareholding governments are: Cook Islands, Fiji, Kiribati, Nauru, New Zealand, Papua New Guinea, Solomon Islands, Tonga, and Western Samoa.

of Kiribati.) Three trunk lines service trade between Australia, New Zealand, and the larger island countries—two of which operate out of New Zealand and the other out of Australia. Two of these routes take approximately 25 days each and the other about 34 days. A feeder service, funded by Australian and New Zealand governments, also operates between Fiji and the two small island countries of Kiribati and Tuvalu. The main operational office is located in Auckland although the designated head office is Apia; the company is registered in Western Samoa.

PFL has had a checkered history, and its capacity to survive has been threatened on more than one occasion. In the past, its performance has been undermined by severe undercapitalization and from operating in a highly competitive industry. A strong commitment to regional cooperation in this field by its members, as manifested by a large capital injection in 1983, has helped PFL survive. After making heavy losses in the past, operating profits have been recorded over the past three years and, insofar as its broader mandate is concerned, the PFL appears to have succeeded in some degree in stabilizing freight rates and in maintaining a regular schedule of services. (PFL lowered its freight rates by 4 percent in 1986.) Although PFL stands to make a loss in the current period, reflecting more intensive competition and reduced freight volume from Fiji due largely to the economic repercussions of the 1987 military coups, it is expected that over the long term the line can be self-sustaining.

Recent attempts to consolidate PFL's operations include the establishment of several shipping agencies (Auckland, Christchurch, and Suva), a stevedoring unit (Apia), and two buildings. (The latter is viewed mainly as an investment.)

PFL policy is set by a board of directors elected by shareholding governments and is composed of seven members drawn mostly from the private sector. The chairman of the board reports to the South Pacific Regional Shipping Council on PFL affairs but has little direct contact with the South Pacific Forum and its Secretariat.

Forum Fisheries Agency (FFA)

The FFA was founded in 1979 to foster regional cooperation in fisheries—a major resource for all island countries. Regional cooperation in this area became particularly crucial with the negotiation of the Law of the Sea Convention in the mid-1970s and the subsequent establishment of Exclusive Economic Zones (EEZs) that greatly enhanced the fisheries potential of island countries. Membership is restricted to Forum members and to any other island state whose admission has been approved by the South Pacific Forum. (Earlier proposals to include other Pacific coastal states, including the United States, were rejected because island states could not reach agreement on certain issues, particularly over the refusal of the United States to recognize the island states' rights over the migratory fish species on their fisheries zones.)

FFA's principal functions are to provide advice and related technical services to island member countries so that they can maximize the benefits to themselves from exploiting the fisheries resources of their EEZs. Among the information provided by FFA are data relating to the activities of foreign fishing vessels, tuna catches, trade and price conditions, licensing fees, fishing treaty arrangements, and progress made by member countries to develop processing and other shore facilities. A regional registry of fishing vessels is maintained—a particularly valuable service to members for purposes of managing the collection of license fees.

FFA also services the meetings of the so-called Nauru Group and acts as the administrator of the Fisheries Access Treaty recently negotiated between the United States and 16 Pacific countries.[3] In relation to both these arrangements, FFA provided valuable advice and related support to island countries during negotiations. FFA is currently assisting member countries in negotiating a regional treaty with Japan along lines somewhat similar to the Access Treaty with the U.S.

The membership of FFA is identical with that of the South Pacific Forum except for the inclusion of Palau. An adjunct body—the Fisheries Committee—whose members are drawn from member countries—provides guidance on policy and administrative matters. Headquartered in Honiara, FFA derives the bulk of its funds from Australia and New Zealand and from a variety of international sources.[4]

South Pacific Trade Commission (SPTC)

The SPTC, based in Sydney, was established in 1979 to foster the economic development of South Pacific Forum island countries, through the promotion of trade and investment. Specifically, SPTC was set up to provide a facility for promoting the sale of island products in Australia and for encouraging Australian investment in island countries,

---

[3] The Nauru Group consists of seven countries pledged by an international treaty, "the Nauru Agreement", to cooperate in fisheries matters, particularly in adopting a coordinated approach in negotiations with distant-water fishing nations over the exploitation of tuna. The seven countries are: FSM, Kiribati, the Marshall Islands, Nauru, Palau, Papua New Guinea, and Solomon Islands. The bulk of tuna catches taken within the sea area is controlled by this group. For details on the U.S.-Pacific countries Fisheries Access Treaty see chapter 3.

[4] Australia, New Zealand, and the island countries collectively, each contributes one-third of FFA's regular budget.

particularly through joint ventures. In effect, SPTC acts as a practical facility for effecting some of the basic objectives laid out in SPARTECA. However, SPTC's role is not restricted to promoting Australia as a market and investment source but also extends to any other metropolitan country whose nationals may wish to trade with and invest in Forum island countries.

A variety of approaches is used to promote island exports to Australia—trade displays and exhibitions in the main Australian cities, training in export procedures, seminars, exchange schemes, personal contracts, and attachment to SPTC. Investment assistance is implemented through a process involving the identification of an idea, developing it to the feasibility stage, and even as far as to the identification of an interested entrepreneur. Assistance can also take the form of management support by identifying sources of finance.

Headed by a Senior Trade Commissioner, SPTC reports to the South Pacific Forum through the Forum Secretariat. It is funded by the Australia International Development Assistance Bureau (AIDAB), and its annual budget must be approved by the Forum Secretariat committee.

SPTC's worth as a practical agency for assisting Forum island countries in the export and investment areas appears to be well established. This experience was a factor in persuading New Zealand to establish a similar facility in Auckland in 1988.

South Pacific Applied Geoscience Commission (SOPAC)

Originally called the Committee for Coordination of Joint Prospecting for Mineral Resources in South Pacific Offshore Areas (CCOP/SOPAC), SOPAC was established in 1972 under the auspices of the United Nations. It became an intergovernmental regional organization in 1984. SOPAC has recently developed links with the South Pacific Forum, to which it now reports annually. Membership totals 12 inclusive of Australia, New Zealand, and Guam (by virtue of its association with ESCAP, SOPAC's former sponsoring agency).

SOPAC's main objective is to assist island members in establishing and assessing the presence of mineral deposits and other non-living resources in the sea areas under the maritime jurisdiction of island members. Its coordinating work includes the investigation and collection of basic data on deep seabed minerals (polymetallic manganese nodules, cobalt crusts, and metallic sulfides); seashore minerals (gravel, sand, coral aggregates, insular phosphate, black and precious coral, and placer and detrital gold); hydrocarbon; and wave energy potential. SOPAC is also active in training in the area of marine geology and non-living resources, mapping of seabeds to establish geological features, coastal engineering for development, data management, and dissemination of information.

Responsible for policy and the reviewing of SOPAC's program is a Committee of Representatives, which meets once a year, and whose members are drawn from member governments. (Other interested Pacific island countries can attend these sessions as observers.) Also assisting in formulating SOPAC's research program is a Technical Advisory Group composed of invited experts from all over the world. This group also meets annually.

International support for SOPAC has been strong, particularly from the United Nations Development Program (UNDP), Japan, Australia, France, and New Zealand. Funding support and technical assistance from these and related sources amount to about F$9.0 million per year and funding support for the foreseeable future seems secure. SOPAC members each contribute a modest F$9,800 toward the annual program of expenditure.

South Pacific Regional Environment Program (SPREP)

Regional Cooperation on the environment began in 1976 when the South Pacific Forum directed its Secretariat (SPEC at the time) to consult with the SPC for purposes of preparing proposals for an integrated regional approach to problems of environmental management. Following two technical meetings and a regional conference (entitled Human Environment in the South Pacific), a SPREP action plan was prepared in 1982 and implementation began in 1983. The action plan laid down the essential purpose of SPREP, namely to assist the countries of the SPC region "to maintain and improve their shared environment and to enhance their capacity to provide a present and future resource base to support the needs and maintain the quality of life of the people." Adopted as the basis for a regional comprehensive strategy, the action plan identified at least 60 problem areas that the SPREP Secretariat should consider in developing its work program.

In line with the action plan, SPREP's work program focuses on the following areas: (1) watershed management (soil erosion, sedimentation, poor forest and agriculture policies); (2) inland and coastal water quality monitoring and control (levels of toxicity, flooding); (3) survey and monitoring of coastal ecosystems and their interaction (mangroves, coral and reef communities); (4) study of ocean conditions (monitoring pollution); and (5) review of regulations and use of pesticides. Additionally, SPREP was to attend to specific country requests in the above and related areas, including bird conservation and marine parks.

SPREP's mandate has been extended and strengthened by two further initiatives: the adoption of an Action Strategy for Protected Areas in the South Pacific (1985), and the negotiation of a Convention for the Protection and Development of the Natural Resources of the South Pacific (1986). The convention and its two related protocols—one dealing with cooperation in combatting pollution emergencies and the other with the prevention of pollution caused by radioactive and other hazardous waste dumping—is a milestone with potentially far-reaching implications. The convention also gives a legal underpinning to all future activities of SPREP. For the convention to come into force, ten signatures were needed. France and Western Samoa became the ninth and tenth signatories in the fall of 1990, bringing the convention into operation.

Specific project proposals for SPREP's work program come from three sources: country requests; annual consultative meetings of research and consultative institutes in the region (these institutions have recently formed an Association of South Pacific Environmental Institutions); and the SPREP coordinating committee (comprising representatives of the Forum Secretariat, SPC, the United Nations Environment Program (UNEP), and ESCAP with the Forum Secretariat director as chairman). Implementation of SPREP projects relies heavily on a cooperative approach especially with regional research and funding institutions. The implementation process lays a heavy emphasis on training and the involvement of local organizations and people.

SPREP services all Pacific island countries and is hosted by the SPC. Its work program is submitted to the South Pacific Forum and the South Pacific Conference for endorsement. Just over 40 percent of its funds come from UNEP (which identifies SPREP as one of its "regional seas" areas) and the bulk of the remainder derives from the voluntary contributions of members. Total contributions to SPREP currently amount to approximately $1.2 million (1987).

The year 1990 saw SPREP becoming a separate entity with links to the South Pacific Forum similar to those enjoyed by FFA and SOPAC.

Pacific Islands Development Program (PIDP)

PIDP represents an initiative with regional dimensions in the field of research, education, and training. PIDP was established in 1980 following the First Pacific Islands Conference hosted earlier in the same year by the East-West Center and concerned with a variety of development issues under the general theme "Development the Pacific Way." Organized as part of the East-West Center's twentieth anniversary commemorative activities, this conference was promoted partly by the Center's conviction that more should be done for the small island states of the South Pacific.

Membership of the Pacific Islands Conference embraces all island countries regardless of political status as well as several metropolitan countries including Australia, New Zealand, and France. PIDP conducts research and training in areas of development identified by Pacific island leaders themselves. Research is conducted cooperatively, with an emphasis on results the island leaders can use in policy formation and in choosing suitable development strategies. PIDP also acts as the secretariat for the Pacific Islands Conference, which is held every five years, and two committees—the Standing Committee and the Program Planning Committee.

The Standing Committee was established by the conference to provide guidance and support to PIDP and to review progress in implementing the research program endorsed by the conference. The Standing Committee meets at least once a year and is composed of eight Pacific island leaders normally representing heads of government. The Program Planning Committee consists of representatives of seven island countries and assists in formulating PIDP's work program and in raising research funds.

PIDP has conducted projects in such areas as appropriate government systems, disaster preparedness and rehabilitation, energy, indigenous business development, and regional cooperation.

In addition to a core contribution to the regular budget from the East-West Center, funding support has been secured from several metropolitan countries, international agencies, and Pacific island countries. PIDP's total expenditure amounts to nearly $1.0 million per year.

APPENDIX 3
Exchange Rates
Per U.S. Dollar, 1983–1987

Year	Australian Dollar (F$)	NZ Dollar (NZ$)	Fijian Dollar (F$)	PNG Kina (K)	Solomon Islands (SI$)	Tongan Paaga (T$)	Western Samoan Tala (WS$)	Pacific Financial Community Franc (FCFP)	Vanuatu Vatu (Vatu)
1983	1.09	1.47	1.00	0.82	1.12	1.08	1.49	137	97
1984	1.13	1.73	1.07	0.89	1.26	1.14	1.81	160	100
1985	1.38	1.98	1.15	0.95	1.40	1.36	2.12	165	105
1986	1.50	1.91	1.16	0.96	1.98	1.50	2.19	—	116
1987	1.43	1.60	1.29	0.88	2.00	1.39	2.05	—	111

— not available

Note: Figures for 1983 to 1985 are averages of bank exchange rates prevailing over the year; for 1986, they represent end of year averages; and for 1987, the rates apply to the month of September.

Sources: South Pacific Commission (1988); Asian Development Bank (1987); International Monetary Fund (1988).

Index

Bold numerals in the index indicate an island profile, and italic numerals identify a corresponding map.

Agriculture, 8, 9, 43, 51–52
Airlines, 76
American Samoa, 4, 5, 74, *112*, **113**
  colonization of, 16
  fisheries, 9, 45, 52, 53
  foreign trade, 46–47
  government, 24
  per capita income, 45
ANZUS nations, 88–89, 90
Asian Development Bank (ADB), 77
Asia-Pacific Economic Cooperation (APEC), 62, 107, 108–109
Association of Southeast Asian Nations (ASEAN), 62, 67, 104–107, 108
Australia, 88–90
  colonies, 16, 18
  foreign aid from, 48–49, 51
  and regional cooperation, 59, 65, 66, 69, 71, 72, 75, 76
  trade in the Pacific, 46, 48, 57, 58

Banking, 76–77
Bavadra, Timoci, 31–32
Bougainville Island, 43
  and secession, 27, 35–36
Bush, George, 89, 98

Canada, 73
Canberra Agreement, 69
Caroline Islands. *See* Federated States of Micronesia (FSM)
China, 91, 97
Chirac, Jacques, 30, 99
Colonization, 15–19
  and self-determination, 18–19, 98–100
Compacts of Free Association (CFA), 19, 50, 98
Cook Islands, 5, 70, *114*, **115**
  colonization of, 16, 27
  exports, 47, 48
  foreign aid to, 50
  foreign policy, 84
  government, 22, 23, 25
  per capita income, 46
  politics, 21
  resources, 4, 8–9
  tourism, 55

Easter Island (Rapa Nui), 2
East-West Center, 74–75, 106, 164
  and Honolulu Summit, 89, 98
Ebeye islet, 5
Economic development, 5–9, 57, 59–62, 84, 109–110
  exports, 46–48
  foreign aid, 48–51
  foreign investment, 44–45
  manufacturing, 44
  mining, 43–44, 45
  per capita incomes, 45–46
  primary sector, 43
  problems of, 11–12, 39–43
Education, 65, 69, 73–74, 76
Ellice Islands. *See* Tuvalu
European Community (EC), 46, 49
Exclusive Economic Zones (EEZs), 3, 8, 9, 93–95, 159

Federated States of Micronesia (FSM), 4, 91, *116*, **117**
  colonization of, 16
  government, 19, 22, 23–24
Fiji, 4, 18, 59, 80, *118*, **119**
  colonization of, 16
  coups, 31–33
  exports, 44, 46, 52, 53, 54, 56
  foreign policy, 84, 87, 91, 92
  government, 20–21
  and Pacific regionalism, 70, 71, 76
  per capita income, 45–46
  politics, 21, 28
  population, 5
  resources, 8, 55
  tourism, 45, 55
Fisheries, 8, 52–53, 93–96, 159–160
  and treaties, 58, 87, 92, 95, 160
Flosse, Gaston, 29
Foreign policies, 83–85, 100–101
  and regional institutions, 87, 155–164
Forestry products, 53–54
Forum Fisheries Agency (FFA), 53, 72, 76
  as treaty negotiator, 87, 95, 159–160

167

France, 97
  colonies, 15, 18
  foreign aid from, 48-49, 50, 87
  and Pacific regionalism, 65, 66, 73, 75, 90-91
  territories, 24, 25, 30, 98-100
  trade in the Pacific, 46, 48
Free Papua Movement, 28
French Polynesia, 4, 90, 120, 121
  exports, 47, 48
  foreign aid to, 49
  government, 24, 25
  and independence movement, 28-29, 100
  per capita income, 45
  resources, 8
  tourism, 55

Ganilau, Ratu Sir Penaia, 32
Geography, 3-5
Germany, colonies, 15, 16, 27
Guam, 4-5, 122, 123
  colonization of, 15
  government, 24
  land tenure, 27
  per capita income, 45
  resources, 9
  tourism, 55

Hawaiian Islands, 1-2
Hu Yaobang, 91

Indonesia, 16, 85, 87, 106
Industries, 56-57
Irian Jaya, 1, 16, 28, 85

Japan, 16, 46, 94, 103
  foreign aid from, 50
  and Pacific interests, 13, 73, 91-92, 95
Johnston Atoll, 2, 97-98

Kiribati, 5, 124, 125
  colonization of, 16, 27
  foreign policy, 84, 92, 94
  government, 18, 20, 22
  per capita income, 45, 46
  resources, 4-5, 8-9
Kuini, Adi, 32
Kuranari, Tadashi, 92

Lafleur, Jacques, 30, 99
Land tenure, 26-27, 42
League of Nations, 16, 91
Libya, 86
Lini, Walter, 33, 35, 86
Lomé Convention, 49, 58

Malaysia, 87, 104, 105
Mara, Ratu Sir Kamisese K.T., 31, 32-33, 87
  and the Lae Rebellion, 75, 156n1
Marshall Islands, 4-5, 126, 127
  colonization of, 16
  government, 19, 22, 23
  resources, 9
Matignon Accords, 99
Melanesia, 4, 5, 17
  federation movement of, 85, 86
  political divisions, 26, 28, 79
Melanesian Spearhead Group, 28, 79, 85-86, 87
Micronesia, 4, 15-16, 28
  social structure, 17, 26
Midway Island, 2
Mineral resources, 8, 54-55, 56
Mitterrand, François, 99

Nakayama, Toshiwo, 91
Nauru, 4-5, 70, 128, 129
  colonization of, 16
  foreign policy, 84
  government, 18, 20, 22
  land use, 27
  per capita income, 45
  resources, 9
Nauru Group, 160
Netherlands, 65
  colonies, 15, 16
Netherlands New Guinea. See Irian Jaya
New Caledonia, 4, 9-10, 59, 130, 131
  exports, 46, 48
  foreign aid to, 49
  government, 24, 25
  and Kanak independence movement, 28, 29-31, 85, 86, 90, 98-100
  mining, 43-44
  per capita income, 45
  resources, 8
New Guinea, 16. See also Papua New Guinea
New Hebrides, 15, 16. See also Vanuatu
Newly industrialized economies (NIEs), 13, 103-104
New Zealand, 88-90
  and free-association relationships, 22, 23
  and regional cooperation, 58, 65, 66, 69, 71, 72, 75, 76
  territories, 16, 18, 24-25, 27
  trade in the Pacific, 46, 48, 57, 58

Index

Niue, 5, *132*, **133**
  colonization of, 16
  foreign aid to, 50
  foreign policy, 84
  government, 22, 23, 27
  resources, 8–9
Norfolk Island, 2
Northern Marianas, 4–5, 74, *134*, **135**
  colonization of, 16
  government, 19, 22, 23
  per capita income, 45
  resources, 9
  tourism, 55
Nuclear testing, 89, 90, 96–98

Official development assistance (ODA), 48, 50
Oil resources, 8
Ona, Francis, 36

Pacific Basin Development Council (PBDC), 74
Pacific Economic Cooperation Conference (PECC), 107–108
Pacific Forum Line (PFL), 72, 158–159
Pacific Islands Development Program (PIDP), 74, 75, 163–165
Pacific Islands Industrial Development Scheme (PIIDS), 56, 58–59
Pacific Islands Producers Association (PIPA), 70–71
"Pacific Way," 12, 66–67, 72, 85, 87
Palau (Belau), 4–5, *136*, **137**
  colonization of, 16
  foreign aid to, 50–51
  government, 9, 19, 22, 23, 24, 25
  resources, 55
Papua New Guinea (PNG), 3, 5, 17, 55, 56, 59, *138*, **139**
  exports, 44, 46, 48, 51–52, 53, 54, 105
  foreign aid to, 49, 50, 51
  foreign policy, 84–85, 86, 91, 92, 94–95
  government, 18, 20, 21–22, 27, 34–36
  member of Melanesian Spearhead Group, 28, 79, 80
  mining, 8, 35, 43–44, 54–55
  per capita income, 45–46
  population, 5
  resources, 9
Pitcairn Island, 2
Pohiva, Samuel "Akilisi," 26
Political status, 9–11
Polynesia, 4, 5, 17, 79
  political groups, 26, 28
Population, 5–7, 8, 9, 42, 62

Rabuka, Sitiveni, 31, 32, 33
Reagan, Ronald, 19
Regional cooperation, 12–13, 57–59, 62–63, 65–75
  characteristics of, 75–76
  future of, 77–80
  weaknesses of, 76–77
  See also by individual organization
Robati, Pupeke, 25
Rocard, Michel, 99

Salato, E.M., 66
Salii, Lazarus, 25
Sasakawa, Ryoichi, 92
Singapore, 105
Single regional organization (SRO), 70, 79
Sokomanu, George, 34
Solarz, Stephen, 97
Solomon Islands, 3, 5, 16, 45, 56, 59, 74, 100, *140*, **141**
  colonization of, 16
  exports, 46, 52, 53, 54, 105
  and fishing access, 94
  government, 18, 20, 25
Sope, Barak, 33, 34, 86
South Korea, 94, 95
South Pacific Applied Geoscience Commission (SOPAC), 72, 161–162
South Pacific Bureau of Economic Cooperation (SPEC), 65, 71
  See also South Pacific Forum Secretariat
South Pacific Commission (SPC), 1, 53, 79, 155–157
  establishment of, 65, 68, 69–70
South Pacific Conference, 69, 70, 71
South Pacific Forum, 71–73, 75, 77
  and consultations with ASEAN, 105–107
  establishment of, 65, 68, 70–71
  and international relations, 84, 85, 87
  and New Caledonia issue, 99
South Pacific Forum Secretariat, 69, 70, 76, 79, 108, 157–158
  establishment of, 65, 71
  as host of ASEAN meeting, 106
South Pacific Nuclear Free Zone (SPNFZ) Treaty, 92, 96–97
South Pacific Organizations Coordinating Committee (SPOCC), 70
South Pacific Regional Environment Programme (SPREP), 72, 162–163
South Pacific Regional Trade and Economic Cooperation Agreement (SPARTECA), 57–58, 72

South Pacific Trade Commission, 72, 160–161
South Pacific Trade Office, 72, 161
South Tarawa, 5
Soviet Union
  fishing agreements, 13, 88, 92–93, 94–95
  and nuclear testing, 97
Spain, colonies, 15, 16

Taiwan, 91, 94, 95
Tjibaou, Jean-Marie, 29–30, 99
Tokelau, 3, 5, *142*, **143**
  colonization of, 16
  foreign aid to, 50
  government, 24–25
  per capita income, 45
  resources, 4, 8–9
Tonga, 4, 5, 57, 70, 74, *144*, **145**
  colonization of, 16
  exports, 44, 56, 58
  foreign policy, 79, 84, 92
  government, 18, 19–20, 22, 27
  per capita income, 45–46
  politics, 17, 26
  resources, 8
Tourism, 8, 55–56, 57
Trust Territory of the Pacific Islands (TTPI), 19
Tuvalu, 3, 5, *146*, **147**
  colonization of, 16, 18, 27
  foreign policy, 84
  government, 22
  per capita income, 45
  resources, 8–9

UN Convention on the Law of the Sea, 93, 94
UN Development Program (UNDP), 49
United Kingdom
  colonies, 15, 16, 18
  foreign policy, 88
  and nuclear testing, 96–97
  and Pacific regionalism, 65, 72–73, 75
  trade in the Pacific, 46

United Nations, 17, 84, 99
United Nations trusteeships, 5, 16, 18, 24
  dissolution of, 15, 22–23
United States, 94
  colonies, 5, 15–16, 19, 24
  and fishing relations, 95–96
  foreign aid from, 48–49, 50, 51, 88, 89, 95
  and free-association relationships, 22, 23, 98
  and nuclear testing, 89, 96–97
  and regional cooperation, 13, 65, 73, 75
  trade in the Pacific, 46, 48
University of the South Pacific (USP), 65, 69, 73–75, 76

Vanuatu, 4, *148*, **149**
  colonization of, 15, 16
  exports, 54
  foreign policy, 86, 95
  member of Melanesian Spearhead Group, 28, 79, 85
  politics, 18–19, 21, 33–35
  resources, 8, 55

Wallis and Futuna, 4, 28, *150*, **151**
  foreign aid to, 50
Wellington Convention, 95, 96
Western Samoa, 4, 5, 70, 91, *152*, **153**
  colonization of, 9, 16
  education, 74
  exports, 54
  government, 17–18, 20, 24, 25
  per capita income, 45
  politics, 21, 25–26
  resources, 8
  tourism, 55
West Irian. *See* Irian Jaya
Wingti, Paias, 85

About the Authors

RICHARD W. BAKER is a Research Associate in the East-West Center's Program on International Economics and Politics. He holds a Master's degree in Public Affairs from the Woodrow Wilson School, Princeton University. From 1967 to 1987 he was a career officer in the U.S. Foreign Service, serving in Singapore, Indonesia, and Australia and at the Department of State in Washington, D.C. His areas of interest and specialization include Southeast Asia, Australia/New Zealand, and Oceania as well as Asia-Pacific regionalism.

TE'O I. J. FAIRBAIRN is a Consultant specializing in Pacific Island Economics and is an Adjunct Research Associate in the East-West Center's Program on International Economics and Politics. He has a Ph.D. in Pacific History from the Australian National University and a Master's degree in Economics from the University of Washington, Seattle. Dr. Fairbairn has done consulting work for the Pacific Islands Development Program, the Commonwealth Secretariat, UNCTAD, UNESCO, ESCAP, the IMF as well as for several island governments.

SHEREE A. GROVES is a business consultant, and was a Research Associate with the Program on International Economics and Politics. She has a Master's degree in International Policy Studies from the Monterey Institute of International Studies and a Bachelor's degree in Asian Studies. She specializes in joint venture development in the People's Republic of China. Ms. Groves' areas of research interest include East Asian international relations and economics.

CHARLES E. MORRISON is Director of the Program on International Economics and Politics at the East-West Center. Dr. Morrison received his Ph.D. from the School of Advanced International Studies (SAIS) at Johns Hopkins University specializing in Southeast Asian international relations. His areas of interest and specialization include the international relations of Asia, U.S.-Japan relations, and U.S. foreign, economic, and trade policies.